ELECTRONIC IRAN

New Directions in International Studies

Patrice Petro, Series Editor

The New Directions in International Studies series focuses on transculturalism, technology, media, and representation, and features the innovative work of scholars who explore various components and consequences of globalization, such as the increasing flow of peoples, ideas, images, information, and capital across borders. Under the direction of Patrice Petro, the series is sponsored by the Center for International Education at the University of Wisconsin–Milwaukee. The center seeks to foster interdisciplinary and collaborative research that probes the political, economic, artistic, and social processes and practices of our time.

For a list of titles in the series, see the last page of the book.

ELECTRONIC IRAN

*The Cultural Politics of
an Online Evolution*

Niki Akhavan

RUTGERS UNIVERSITY PRESS
NEW BRUNSWICK, NEW JERSEY, AND LONDON

Library of Congress Cataloging-in-Publication Data

Akhavan, Niki, 1975–
    Electronic Iran : the cultural politics of an online evolution / Niki Akhavan.
        pages cm. — (New directions in international studies)
    Includes bibliographical references and index.
    ISBN 978–0–8135–6193–6 (hbk. : alk. paper) — ISBN 978–0–8135–6192–9
(pbk. : alk. paper) — ISBN 978–0–8135–6194–3 (ebk.)
        1. Online social networks—Political aspects—Iran. 2. Internet and activism—
Iran. 3. Mass media and nationalism—Iran. I. Title.

    HM742.A4294 2013
    006.7'54—dc23
                                                                            2012051442

A British Cataloging-in-Publication record for this book is available from the
British Library.

Visit our website: http://rutgerspress.rutgers.edu

Manufactured in the United States of America

CONTENTS

ACKNOWLEDGMENTS

When I first became interested in digital media and transnational Iranian political culture as an aspiring graduate student, neither Iran nor the Internet were the hot topics they have since become. If it were not for the University of California at Santa Cruz's History of Consciousness Program and their openness to interdisciplinary projects from off the beaten track, I likely would not have been able to do the work that was necessary to lay the foundation for this book. I was honored to have extraordinary teachers and colleagues in Santa Cruz who continue to amaze me with all that they achieve. I owe special thanks to James Clifford, Barbara Epstein, and Neferti Tadiar.

These are not easy times to speak or write about Iran. Throughout the years when this book was in progress, many friends, colleagues, and mentors whose scholarship focuses on Iran or the Middle East more broadly have provided moral and intellectual support and encouraged me to carry on with my research in the face of numerous political pressures. I wish to thank Roksana Bahramitash, Alireza Doostdar, Suzanne Gauch, Behrooz Ghamari-Tabrizi, Eric Hooglund, Amy Kallander, Fatemeh Keshavarz, Pedram Khosronejad, Hossein Khosrowjah, Mana Kia, Targol Mesbah, Minoo Moallem, Shadi Mokhtari, Babak Rahimi, Najat Rahman, Sima Shakhsari, Ted Swedenburg, and Will Youmans.

I owe a great debt of gratitude to numerous participants on the Iranian Internet who have shared their knowledge and experiences with me in informal spaces online and off. I would like to thank all the Web site administrators, bloggers, journalists, human rights activists, and social media celebrities who have been my interlocutors in the course of this project. I am especially grateful to those who engaged with me despite our starkly differing views.

This work was made possible with financial support from The Catholic University of America. I am thankful to the dean of Arts and Sciences, Larry Poos, for his valuable advice and for the resources he has provided that helped me develop my research and complete this book.

I am very lucky to be a part of a truly collegial and supportive department where I can honestly say that my colleagues are also my friends. The senior members of my department, Stephen McKenna and Alexander Russo, have been very patient and generous in answering my numerous queries about publishing and academic life in general. To my other colleagues, Jennifer Fleeger, Abby Moser, and Maura Ugarte, I am inspired by the work you do and have learned a great deal from our conversations over the years. I am grateful for the daily support of our department's administrative assistant, Tonya Oben. Thanks also to my research assistant, Sarah Spalding, for her help in proofreading and formatting the manuscript.

I would like to thank the editors, staff, and readers at Rutgers University Press. I am grateful to series editor Patrice Petro and editor-in-chief Leslie Mitchner for their enthusiasm about this project and for guiding me through the process of its completion. I would also like to thank Lisa Boyajian, Marilyn Campell, and Suzanne Kellam for their work and their patience in answering my questions during various stages of manuscript preparation. Special thanks go to Kate Babbitt for the many astute queries and helpful suggestions she made in editing the book.

I am blessed with a large and wonderful extended family whose support has sustained me over the years. Special thanks go to my parents, Shahla Rahmani and Masoud Akhavan, and my brother, Naumdar Akhavan, for their constant encouragement and love. Finally, to my partner, Raed Jarrar: this project would never have been completed without your loving support and incisive feedback. Thank you for pushing me for clarity when I hid behind ambiguities, for your technical assistance, and for maintaining your sense of humor during my more dramatic writing moments.

ELECTRONIC IRAN

INTRODUCTION

Nascent Networks

The sense of excitement that accompanied the introduction of the Internet in the 1990s to the general public continues to inspire hopeful speculation about its potentials more than a decade into the new millennium. In the case of Iran, the advent of and rapid developments in Internet technologies coincided with a number of tumultuous shifts inside the country and its immediate neighborhood, intensifying the sense that positive transformations were on the horizon. During the more than fifteen years since resident and Diaspora Iranians have taken to the Internet, a number of remarkable changes have occurred. From producing and participating in one of the most vibrant blogospheres during the early days of Web 2.0 to capturing and disseminating audiovisual content during the massive demonstrations following the June 2009 presidential election, Iranians have established a place online and have captured international attention in so doing.[1]

Yet the digital era has not been without its disappointments. While new technologies continue to be heralded for their utility in confronting state powers, the ruling structure in Iran survived a series of challenges that the Internet magnified, in the process emboldening some of its most reactionary elements. In addition, government entities took to digital media, using them to disseminate cultural products that strengthened the government's position. Other segments not linked to the Iranian government, from independent users to those whose participation is enabled by support from other states, have also revealed a number of troubling tendencies such as cultivating exclusionary ideologies or using their presence on the Internet to inflate

1

the extent to which they represent Iranian society.[2] In short, although popular accounts proliferate about the Internet and its promising implications for Iranian culture, politics, and society, the field of analysis remains rich and largely unexplored. Focusing on the years spanning from roughly 1998 through 2012, this book examines often-overlooked terrains of the Iranian Internet. I examine which elements have been discounted and why, revealing a complex and contradictory landscape that presents reasons for both concern and celebration.

The Iranian Internet provides my conceptual framework as well as the site of analysis. It is not "Iranian" in any straightforward way, nor is it confined to a technology or space captured by the all-encompassing term "the Internet." It is more than simply "Iranian" because it flows across national borders and includes material written about Iran in both Persian and other languages. It is more than simply "the Internet" because it follows the converging connections between online and offline and identifies how they often reciprocally shape one another. The Iranian Internet is not one but many places. It is frequented and inhabited by geographically and ideologically dispersed participants, and it is always contested, always changing.

My conceptualization of the Iranian Internet has been influenced by ethnographies and works in media history that offer insights for analyzing technologies at the moment when they are still "new." The ethnographic scholarship that assessed the Internet in its early years has been particularly useful. Relatively early on, ethnographers argued that any examination of the Internet should be grounded in the material realities that give rise to new technologies and shape the ways they are used. These accounts emphasized the importance of treating the Internet as both a site and a product of cultural production (Hine 2000; Miller and Slater 2000).

Understanding the Internet as a "new" medium, especially in light of the rapidity of its developments, poses difficulties in methods and definition. At times, the progression from emerging to new to established media seems to occur before one has had the opportunity to grasp the technology in question. What is emergent media at one moment becomes merely new in the next and may be categorized as established soon thereafter. Influential works in media history have demystified the notion of "new" media. They have stressed the importance of assessments of new media that ground their analysis in the specific and contested social, political, and legal conditions of a technology's emergence; that pay attention to how diverse users play a role in defining and assimilating a new medium; and that highlight the continuities and relationships between new and previously existing technologies (Altman 2004; Gitelman 2006; Marvin 1988).

If this book is cautious in its assessment of emerging technologies and media practices, it has taken cues from findings in several disciplines. Speaking specifically about diasporas, Benedict Anderson was prescient in warning against uses of new telecommunication technologies for the purpose of intensifying absolutist nationalist sentiments (Anderson 1998). Ethnographers confirmed Anderson's insight, drawing attention to the ways that the transnational medium of the Internet has been used to strengthen—rather than to challenge—nationalism and other exclusionary ideologies (Ang 2001; Lal 1999; Ong 2003; Sorenson and Matsuoka 2001). Since these early works, cautionary accounts have emerged in other fields. The most visible of these has been the work of legal scholars, who have found an audience among mainstream readers. This work ranges from those that present somewhat alarmist claims about the destructive consequences of the Internet for democracy and education (Sunstein 2007) to those that may critique the trajectory of new media developments but offer prescriptions for how to return to the right path (Lessig 2001; Lessig 2004; Zittrain 2008). While my approach and my assessments do not fall in any one place along the spectrum of pessimistic or utopian assessments of the Internet, I share with Lawrence Lessig and Jonathan Zittrain a sense that problematic developments in digital media can provide lessons about achieving its promising potential in the future.

If the Internet as object of study poses challenges arising from its fluidity as a site of analysis and the speed of technological developments, examining Iranian politics and culture are rife with equal difficulties. Both Iran's state powers and members of oppositional groups are notoriously factionalized, and shifts occur regularly but unpredictably. Fields of cultural production are similarly dynamic: organs of the state, government-supported entities, dissident artists and activists, and apolitical individuals and institutions who have competing visions about the nature and identity of the Iranian state and society participate as content producers. These complexities are mirrored and intensified through new media technologies and require analyses that are in tune with the richness of media developments and the social and political contexts in which they are received. Annabelle Sreberny and Gholam Khiabany have suggested in their book on the blogosphere that understanding the digital turn in Iranian media requires that it be assessed in the context of previous and existing policies, technologies, and political dynamics (Sreberny and Khiabany 2011).

Other important factors that are relevant to a study of the Iranian Internet can be found in Iranian studies scholarship that has addressed various media, cultural products, and/or forms of state power. Recognizing the importance of images and visual cultures in contemporary Iran, Roxanne Varzi and Negar Mottahedeh have examined a range of representational practices and their relevance to expressions of state power and resistance (Mottahedeh 2008; Varzi 2006). Highlighting the gendered constructions of notions of community and nation in postrevolution Iran, Minoo Moallem has provided extensive analysis of written and visual texts (Moallem 2005). Her assessment of fundamentalism in Iran provides an important guide for my attempts to make sense of the relationship between the Iranian state and emergent media. Among the rare few whose work on Iran and media explicitly calls for an analysis of how state powers actively use—rather than merely repress and disrupt—communication technologies, Gholam Khiabany has uncovered the complex and often-contradictory relationship of the Iranian state to various forms of media (Khiabany 2010).

In tune with Khiabany's approach, which acknowledges repressive government tactics vis-à-vis media but reveals a range of proactive uses of new technologies, I trace developments in the state's engagement with the Internet from the dawn of Web 1.0 to the era of social media. Authority in Iran is distributed unevenly in dynamic and contested ways, and parallel and redundant institutions compete with each other. My use of the term "state" or "state powers" is not meant to elide the complexities of the ruling structure or to reify it as a singular entity that stands against another singular entity captured by terms such as "the people" or "the opposition." It is simply shorthand that allows me to follow how various elements of the ruling structure—specifically those that dominate and have the most to lose in power struggles—have been active in using media technologies to build and entrench their presence both online and off.

The history of the Iranian state's involvement with the Internet reveals a curious combination of tactics. On the one hand, the government has developed the telecommunications infrastructure needed for the Internet to function. The state and its affiliates (such as the Revolutionary Guards) are also the main owners and investors in the telecommunication and information industry infrastructure (Sreberny and Khiabany 2011). It also grants permission to and sets the conditions for privately owned Internet service providers (ISPs). In a basic sense, the state has complete control over the Internet inside Iran: if it chooses to, it can collapse the entire system. For example, after the disputed 2009 election, the state did not shut down the Internet. For the most part, its mechanisms for controlling the Internet have been restricted to filtering content and limiting speed; the latter is a favorite tactic during periods of actual or anticipated political upheaval.[3] Other repressive forms of power have included surveillance and the harassment and in some cases detention of Internet users.

The explanation for why the ruling establishment has not chosen complete technology blackout can be found in other aspects of its relationship to new media. Iranian state institutions and actors have long been savvy users of various forms of media, and their responses to digital technologies have been no different. The Iranian state has a two-pronged strategy for dealing with digital media: a well-documented set of repressive mechanisms that functions alongside a vast but largely overlooked set of practices for actively using the Internet as a site for producing and disseminating favorable political speech and cultural products. These two complementary prongs mostly appear to operate independently: that is to say, without reference to one another. Yet the relationships and interconnections between them become evident in times of tumult. Indeed, not long after the post-2009 election demonstrations, which was arguably the biggest crisis of legitimacy for the Islamic Republic since its founding after the 1979 revolution, the state articulated a strategy for a "soft war" that indicates the explicit coming together of heretofore parallel approaches to both new media and new cultural products.

Considering the digital media activities of state powers, state actors, and supporters of the state constitutes only one line of inquiry in my analysis of aspects of the Iranian Internet that are overlooked, unexamined, and/or unappreciated. These include voices and topics that are ripe for analysis but that get sidelined because of the ideology of content producers or, more frequently, assumptions about the ideologies of content producers. Uncovering these elements of the Iranian Internet requires a deep exploration of Internet-enabled transnational expressions of combat and collaboration in a range of venues, including blogs, audiovisual posts, the comments sections of popular Web sites, and social media sites. In all the periods I consider here, the many examples of translocal and transnational connectivity offer much to celebrate. Indeed, given the geographical and ideological diversity, at times the mere fact that the Iranian Internet provides a gathering place for those with disparate views is remarkable. Even more noteworthy are the rare instances when participants agree that their Internet-based collaborations have been successful or when competing points of view are settled in a way that approximates exchanges in an ideal public sphere.

Chapter 1, "Reembodied Nationalisms," begins with the formative years of the Internet in the late 1990s. Inside Iran, these years coincided with the surprising victory of the reformists, who had been supported in large part by a youthful population that was either too young to remember or was not yet born during the 1979 revolution. Young people who were voting for the first time and Iranians who were newly energized by the shifting political terrain were also among the earliest participants on the Internet. Yet it was members of the Iranian Diaspora—particularly those who were writing in a non-Iranian language—who initially dominated the Iranian Internet and influenced discourses and practices online. Technical proficiency is largely responsible for the strong early presence of Diaspora members; they had access to the resources and the language skills required to take full advantage of the new technology. While the development of infrastructure inside Iran and the appearance of Unicode for Persian fonts would soon shift the balance, analysis of the first years of the Iranian Internet requires an assessment of the role of Diaspora in particular.

This chapter uncovers sites of intense activity and analyzes what they reveal about the Iranian Internet in its infancy. Issues related to the naming of the Persian Gulf were among the first to catalyze transnational mobilizations online, a process that pushed participants to explore the new opportunities digital technologies offered. The question of how that body of water is labeled in various international contexts has consistently raised the passions of resident and Diaspora Iranians no matter where they fall on the political spectrum. Online responses to the Persian Gulf issue date to the 1990s. An early instance of Internet-enabled transnational collaboration among Iranians unfolded in 1996 on the pages of the Web site The Iranian (or Iranian.com, as it also came to be called). Following the case study of the Persian Gulf issue, the chapter traces the genesis of new modes of political action and cultural production that emerged alongside the rapid development of new technologies, from the static pages of the early Internet to the participatory spaces of Web 2.0. It shows that while digital media may make new forms of collective action possible, they are also conducive to the reemergence and cultivation of exclusionary ideologies, particularly those pertaining to nationalism and national identity that thrive on gendered and racialized constructions.

Internet-enabled activism around the Persian Gulf also provides a lens for examining how state actors became visible participants on the Iranian Internet. The chapter shows how government entities and officials eagerly entered the fray, promoting the production of particular kinds of content online and in some cases even co-opting oppositional Internet-based movements. Instances of Persian Gulf activism, particularly the participation of the state, also draw attention to important features of the Iranian Internet. New technologies may be used to both open new spaces for activism and magnify steps taken offline, thus giving an advantage to those who have the capacity to mobilize in multiple spaces. Governments and their institutions, which have access to resources that include other forms of media, are well placed to use new media to enhance their power, a fact that is often unnoticed in assessments of the Internet as a vehicle for challenging state power.

Against this backdrop of the early and transitional years of the Web, Chapter 2, "Uncharted Blogospheres," focuses attention on the heyday of the Iranian blogosphere, which roughly spans from 2003 to 2008. Weblogistan, as it is known to Iranian users, is among the most celebrated and written-about aspects of the Iranian Internet. Both popular and academic accounts have made a convincing case that the Iranian blogosphere is well suited for expressing dissent, for challenging the power structure's favored interpretations of past and present events, and for finding alternate routes of disseminating information. Yet despite its prevalence as a favorite topic, large segments of Weblogistan remain unexamined.

The chapter provides a supplement to existing narratives about Weblogistan from two complementary angles. First, it examines examples from distinct but overlapping categories of blogs that are often either entirely overlooked or only briefly considered in the dominant literature about Weblogistan. These blogs belie a number of misconceptions about Iran and the blogosphere and reflect serious fissures in Iranian society and the political structure. Although they may not present issues from the secular or oppositional perspectives favored by many journalistic accounts of Weblogistan produced outside Iran, the bloggers under consideration do not shrink from using the medium in ways that challenge social and political mores. Second, this chapter considers a number of state-sponsored actions aimed at shaping Weblogistan. The available material on the Iranian blogosphere, particularly reports produced by human rights and nongovernmental organizations, has documented the Iranian government's repressive policies toward the blogosphere such as filtering content, blocking access, and in some cases arresting bloggers. These actions show the ruling system's recognition of the serious challenges Weblogistan may pose. The state-sponsored actions examined in this chapter—including attempts to shape discourses on and about Weblogistan—reveal that it also appreciates the potential of the blogosphere for promoting its own cultural and political agendas.

Chapter 3, "The Movable Image," introduces a new line of inquiry into the intersection of moving image cultures and the Iranian Internet in the years 2004–2010. It focuses on material pertaining to the eight-year war with Iraq, a conflict that continues to have resonance in contemporary Iran and that has engendered a vast and expanding body of cultural products. An emerging body of literature has begun to consider the place of war-related books, posters, murals, and films to the contested processes of defining the Iranian state, Iranian society, and Iranian citizenship. The digital versions of these materials and how they function online, however, have yet to be critically examined. In fact, audiovisual materials on the Iranian Internet in general have not been thoroughly examined. Exceptions include accounts of how activists used digital technologies to capture and circulate audiovisual materials during the protests following the elections of 2009. It is noteworthy that even the moving images produced about the 2009 protests used state-sanctioned tropes of the Iran-Iraq war. This chapter argues that the often-curious manifestations of audiovisual cultural products about the war have been both productive and disruptive for state powers, individuals, and/or organizations with an interest in contemporary uses of the Iran-Iraq war.

Chapter 3 begins with an overview of mostly state-endorsed cultural products about the Iran-Iraq war, focusing on material produced and/or recirculated from 2004 through 2010. In the first years of this period, resources and a certain level of skill were necessary to digitize, upload, and host audiovisual content. This gave the state and institutions affiliated with it an advantage over individual and independent users. This picture significantly changed with the advent of free and global platforms for distributing moving images. The chapter considers state-endorsed uses of offline and virtual content about the war, then the recirculation and repurposing (in part or in full) of these materials on the global platform provided by YouTube. The rise of free video-sharing services has resulted in fascinating examples of how content has been remixed and then debated. Examples range from the incorporation of war materials for seemingly irrelevant causes outside Iran to the recasting of audiovisual content about the Iran-Iraq war to challenge the ruling establishment in Iran. Many of the consequences of the development of YouTube may be explained in terms of its features, especially its social networking elements. Discussions of such features set the foundation for an in-depth examination of social media in chapter 4.

By late 2007, the sheen of blogs and blogging was beginning to dull on the Iranian Internet, and social networking sites were showing signs of becoming more popular among resident and Diaspora Iranians. The migration to social media and the implications of this shift are most evident in relation to Internet content about the disputed 2009 presidential election. Protesters' much-touted uses of social media in the aftermath of the disputed election remain a hallmark example of how these platforms can successfully attract transnational attention and support. Yet the focus on this event has overshadowed the significance of social media in earlier periods. Similar to accounts of past periods of the Iranian Internet, most accounts of social media have limited their assessment of state actors to their repressive activities. While social media created important moments on the Iranian Internet, an assessment of their impact requires us to move beyond their functions during the post-election period.

Chapter 4, "Social Media and the Message," covers the rise of social media in Iran and its dominance on the Iranian Internet from 2006 through 2012. It begins with an overview of the ascendancy of social media, pinpointing factors and debates that had an impact on how social media is used in Iran. The chapter examines two key moments in the surge of social media, both of which illustrate innovative uses of digital media and indicate its pitfalls. The first covers the presidential campaign period of 2009, a time when social media seemed to promise much but a time that was overshadowed by the aftermath of the election. I examine the use of the wildly popular—but mostly ignored—aggregate Web site Friendfeed in the campaign period, highlighting the ways that the service enabled new modes of media practice, social and political exchange, and, for fleeting moments, the emergence of near-ideal public spheres. I then move to a consideration of the post-election era, with a specific focus on the state's responses to the changed realities of the country and the digital spaces to which Iran is linked. In this period, widespread resources were openly allocated to explicitly formulate and implement a systematic approach to the new media landscape under the banner of responding to what the state calls a soft war. The chapter considers the implications of this new phase of the state's complicated relationship to media and cultural products.

The conclusion, "New Media Futures," looks back at the rich but disputed territories of the Iranian Internet. Given the volatility of Iranian and regional politics in the nearly twenty years since the popularization of the Internet, the stakes of knowledge production about

Iran are high. Assessing the Iranian Internet with a framework that captures its contradictions and complexities is crucial in any attempt to understand the consequences of new media technologies for Iranian politics, culture, and society. This includes taking seriously state actors' active uses of digital media for the purposes of cultural production and expansion of state power. If the Iranian Internet that is revealed in this book has its troubling sides, it also contains many laudable manifestations of translocal and transnational exchange, collaboration, and creative action. The book concludes on the positive note of advocating that we view the Iranian Internet through a wider lens while taking lessons from both its faults and its realized potential.

CHAPTER 1

REEMBODIED
NATIONALISMS

The early years of the Iranian Internet, which coincided with the rise of the reform movement in Iran and the expanding information technology bubble of the late 1990s, stirred much excitement among participants and observers alike. With the 1997 presidential victory of the reformists, who largely owed their surprise success to young voters with no lived experience of the 1979 revolution, came hopes about a new kind of politics. Outside Iran, the increasing popularity of the Internet and the boom of dotcom start-ups fueled the sense that great possibilities awaited the Internet enthusiast, especially if that individual had entrepreneurial leanings. The Iranian Internet emerged at a time when a mood of hopefulness buoyed users who were becoming active participants.

It is not surprising that the mood of positive anticipation encompassed issues pertaining to the Diaspora, women, and political activism. The ability of Internet technologies to transcend geographical borders dovetailed with similar claims about the Diaspora in the late 1990s, raising the hope that nationalism and other narrow bases for community formation might give way to more inclusive forms of identification. The Internet seemed poised to transcend other rigid power structures such as those pertaining to gender. In short, new media seemed to provide the perfect ground for initiating innovative social relationships and political activism. All of these possibilities gained extra force when applied to the case of Iran, whose ruling system identifies in religious terms and women's roles within that system are limited.

Members of Iran's vocal and relatively prosperous Diaspora—
particularly those writing in non-Iranian languages—initially dominated the Iranian Internet and were influential in shaping early
practices and discourses. The ascendancy of the Diaspora in this early
period was largely due to a number of technical reasons. For example, members of the Diaspora had better access to the Internet, and
because uniform font codes for Persian were not yet developed, those
who could communicate in the language of their host countries were
at an advantage in being able to participate online. Inside Iran, the
state played an important role in the development of the Internet.
For example, it allowed the construction of the telecommunications
infrastructure necessary for the Internet to function and expand. It
also granted permission for ISPs to provide and set the conditions of
service. But despite the state's formative role, it was individual users
who were most visible in their embrace of the new technology.

With the advent of Web 2.0 in the first years of the new millennium, a series of major shifts become apparent on the Iranian Internet. In this period, material written in Persian, mostly by Iran-based
bloggers, began to appear, signaling the dawn of the blogosphere era.
Organs of the state provided another sign of what was to come. While
Iranian state actors adopted mechanisms for filtering and blocking
sites, they also took to the Internet to participate in the production of
certain types of content and to lay claim to a range of digital materials,
including those that expressed opposition to the ruling structure.

The Internet and Nationalisms

Both the Internet and the concept of Diaspora have inspired optimistic claims about the potential for liberation. The notion of Diaspora
raised hope that the repressive boundaries of nation-states, nations,
and national identities could be challenged and transgressed. This line
was particularly evident in the literature of the early to mid-1990s,
when Diaspora studies enjoyed a surge in attention and knowledge
production. Khachig Tölölyan, who famously referred to Diasporas as
the "exemplary communities of the transnational moment" (Tölölyan
1991, 3), was influential in constructing a conceptual framework
that situates Diasporas beyond the nation-state. In Tölölyan's model,

members of a Diaspora are immune to the mechanisms states use to define the terms of political expression, national identity, and social formation. Similarly, James Clifford stressed the "empowering paradox of diaspora[s]" (Clifford 1997, 269) because of their ability to relate to two or more places when articulating notions of belonging. Other theorists share Clifford's mostly positive view of how the hybridity of the Diasporic condition can allow for identity negotiation (Hall 1990; Mercer 1988).[1]

In the late 1990s and early 2000s, the Internet and its technologies similarly inspired a range of hopeful assessments of its potential, especially in terms of issues of nationalism, national identity, and national borders.[2] Some argued that the shrinking of physical distance would make national borders less relevant and lead individuals to form bonds as members of global rather than national communities (Cairncross 1997). Similarly, the idea that digital media makes it possible for users to form a "virtual community" based on choice rather than on physical or political restrictions was posited early on and continues to be popular among Internet users (Rheingold 1993; Rheingold 2000). In 1997, Nicholas Negroponte, the architect of the One Laptop per Child project who at the time was the director of the MIT Media Laboratory, went so far as to claim that within twenty years, the impact of the Internet would be such that children would "not . . . know what nationalism is."[3]

While these promises remain alluring, Diasporic realities—particularly in intersection with digital media technologies—have offered contrary tendencies. Some members of Diasporic populations use the Internet as a vehicle for promoting nationalism (Eriksen 2007),[4] and the literature includes case studies describing the disturbing outcomes of mobilizations of Internet technologies by Diaspora members. For example, Ien Ang's case study of a diasporic Chinese website has shown the conduciveness of the Internet to ethnic militancy, Vinay Lal has traced the relationship between the Indian Diaspora's use of the Internet and the rise of fundamentalist Hinduism, and John Sorenson and Atsuko Matsuoka have highlighted the resurgence of Absyinnian fundamentalism among the Ethiopian Diaspora online (Ang 2001; Lal 1999; Sorenson and Matsuoka 2001).

Some of the virulence of Internet-enhanced versions of "long-distance nationalisms" may be explained in terms of the Diasporic

condition itself (Anderson 1998, 74). Predating the rise in scholarship about what Sheffer calls "diasporas' militancy" (Sheffer 2003, 5),
Edward Said argued that revolutionary nationalism in exile taps into
the nostalgia of individuals and a group's shared sense of exclusion
from the dominant society, giving meaning to the marginalization
the Diaspora experiences (Said 2000). Studies on Tamils in Norway,
Hindus in Holland, and Pakistanis in the United Kingdom, for example, have noted how dual alienation helps account for the articulation
and appeal of long-distance nationalism (Fuglerud 1999; Jacobsen
and Kumar 2003; Werbner 2001). Attention to digital media is also
key to understanding why online arenas easily cultivate nationalisms.
Paradoxically, Internet technologies produce spaces of togetherness
and exclusion at the same time. While they allow disparately located
individuals to converge in one place, they also provide the means to
bar the participation of those whose views differ from the group that
is gathering. The dangers of the spaces created through practices of
selective inclusion are twofold: because they have the potential to
draw together geographically dispersed participants, they may easily
feed the notion that the dominant views espoused in these spaces represent the views of a wide constituency. In addition, the exclusion of
voices of dissent may fuel a false sense of consensus where none exists.

Some see digital media technologies as a threat to fundamental
elements of democracy, education systems, and social relationships
(Carr 2010; Sunstein 2002; Sunstein 2007). Some of these dystopic
warnings appear to be as exaggerated as the utopianism of early celebrations of the Internet era. However, simultaneously considering the
celebrations of new technologies and the concerns of alarmists allows
for the emergence of more nuanced accounts of the social and cultural
impact of digital media.

Although the increasing diversity of viewpoints in assessments of
Internet technologies is a welcome development, gender is a largely
unintegrated component of such accounts, even as the literature
on nationalisms offers insightful arguments about the importance
of gender analysis. Making steady dents in the vast literature on
nationalism, feminist scholars have brought attention to the centrality of gender in the construction of nationalism and national
identity (Kandiyoti 1991; Kandiyoti 2000; Nagel 1998; Walby 1996;

Yuval-Davis 1997). Similar inroads have been made in scholarship on Iran: a number of works cover historical and recent formulations of the nation, national identity, and nationalism using analysis that highlights the role of gender (De Groot 1993; Moallem 2005; Najmabadi 1998; Najmabadi 2005).

These three topics—how people use developments in new technologies, the role of nationalism in online mobilizations, and the centrality of gender to such mobilizations—converge in the debates about the Persian Gulf I consider in this chapter. They show that while participants on the newly formed Iranian Internet used new technologies creatively to promote collaboration, the Internet was also a place where troubling constructions of nationalism and national unity emerged.

CLAIMING THE PERSIAN GULF: ORIGINS OF A CONFLICT ONLINE

From its early years, the Iranian Internet has been conducive to the propagation of nationalisms, and many of the successful mobilizations it has generated have been fueled by nationalist sentiments. Ironically, the transnational connections the Internet makes possible do not necessarily translate to a transcending of national boundaries; in fact, they often work to entrench them. And while the Internet may facilitate the coming together of geographically dispersed individuals, nationalism is often the glue that precipitates and maintains such transnational connections. Indeed, often the most intense instances of Internet-enabled actions and those that participants perceive to be successful uses of digital media depend heavily on nationalism and nationalist sentiments.

These tendencies are best illustrated by one of the earliest and most consistent examples of transnational mobilizations on the Iranian Internet: the debate about the name of the Persian Gulf. Few issues that have engendered widespread responses in the online Iranian community have been more explosive and have had more longevity than this one. The controversy is related to the appearance of the name "Arabian Gulf" for the Persian Gulf. This term has been increasingly used not only in the region among Arabic speakers but internationally as well. The use of "Arabian Gulf" to describe the body of water—even if it is used with rather than as a substitution for the label "Persian Gulf"—has generated online activity among resident and Diasporic Iranians alike.

Although the question of the proper way to refer to the Persian Gulf is often linked to the contemporary political situation in any given moment of perceived crisis, the core issues of concern remain relatively stable, thus providing a constant for measuring how developments in digital technologies are used. It is a useful case study not only for examining the relationship between nationalism and the Internet but also for tracing broader changes on the Iranian Internet as it transitioned from being largely the domain of members of the Iranian Diaspora to a more diverse arena made up of both resident users and members of the Diaspora and both state and nonstate actors. Similarly, as one of the few issues that agitates a wide spectrum of individuals, no matter what their political persuasion and/or where they are located, it provides an opportunity to begin uncovering the diversity of the Iranian Internet. Finally, following the mobilizations around the issue of the name for the Persian Gulf illustrates the involvement of the Iranian state, showing that the state's role goes far beyond simply obstructing access to new technologies, contrary to the bulk of analysis about the Iranian Internet. In fact, the state not only actively uses these technologies but also often co-opts the efforts of those who are trying to use the Internet as an expression of opposition to state policies.

The early development of the Iranian Internet and the mobilizations around the name for the Persian Gulf are best captured in two periods. The first begins in the second half of the 1990s, at the cusp of the popularization of Internet technologies, and carries through roughly the first years of the new millennium.[5] At this time, Diasporic and non-Iranian languages dominated the Iranian Internet for two main reasons: the infrastructure for Internet access was not yet widely available in Iran, and Persian character sets had not yet been developed. During the second stage of the early years, static Web sites continued to play a large role in the virtual landscape but were soon overtaken by Web 2.0 technologies. Developments in Iran's telecommunications infrastructure and an increase in the number of private ISP providers made possible widespread participation within the country. This transitional phase is also characterized by the increasing dominance of the Persian language on the Iranian Internet and the open participation of the state in online arenas.

The starting point of the online responses to the Persian Gulf issue goes back to the late 1990s. This early instance—which may indeed be the first such instance—of Internet-enabled transnational mobilizations among Iranians unfolded in 1996 on the Web site The Iranian (or Iranian.com, as it also came to be called). In 1995, when it was founded, Iranian.com was a no-frills, static site that was typical of the early phases of Web 1.0. However, it did allow readers to interact through a discussion bulletin. In less than one year, the site established itself as a popular and primarily English-language online forum for mostly Diasporic Iranians. Over the years, it has become a hybrid site that includes both edited and user-generated content.[6]

The catalyst for activism came in the form of a letter to the site by a reader who had recently flown on KLM and was incensed to discover that the electronic in-flight map used the term "Arabian Gulf" instead of "Persian Gulf." Taking advantage of The Iranian's broad reach, he used the site to call on "all patriotic people to boycott KLM flights."[7] This simple request, expressed on a forum that drew the participation of geographically dispersed Iranians, received an immediate and passionate response. Readers of the forum began registering their complaints with KLM, many of them using the Internet to communicate with the company. Significantly, many heeded the call to action, reproducing the text of their complaints on the forum provided by Iranian.com. The Web site thus had a magnifying effect: participants shared what they had done, gave one another feedback on what to say and how to say it, and offered advice about what should be done and how best to do it. A heated discussion developed about the importance of the name "Persian Gulf," the broader ramifications of a possible name change, and the best way to address the issue.

Less than two weeks after the original poster complained about the issue, KLM announced that it would change its in-flight software. This development was celebrated in the online forum. The sense of accomplishment was so great that Iranian.com eventually memorialized the action by gathering many of the posts to the forum and archiving them under a section dedicated to the debate.[8]

Although KLM responded quickly in a way that satisfied the site's participants, the moment of perceived crisis was short lived and the debate it engendered was limited. Yet this first spark of transnational activism is significant for a number of reasons, including the fact that it inspired other mobilizations around the same issue. The activism was initiated and sustained online in ways that tapped into the full capacity of available technologies. A convergence of new and old media was apparent as users wrote e-mails, made phone calls, and sent faxes, sharing and sometimes reproducing the texts of their communications with those they had contacted. A public posting by an individual sparked the debate and a grassroots effort sustained the action that followed. This contrasts with later phases of the Iranian Internet, when it increasingly became a site where states found ways of openly or covertly participating in the shaping of online arenas.

This brief flurry of activity provides a preview of what is at stake in the debates about the Persian Gulf and how the Internet may function to filter dissenting views, thus creating spaces where nationalisms can flourish more easily and become more exclusionary. While the participants demonstrated innovation in using the full capacity of the available technologies to achieve what the original poster called for, the discussions stayed within the familiar framework of nationalism. A few questioned the zeal of the participants by recommending the use of multiple names, suggesting other priorities to rally around, and/or mocking the importance that was accorded the topic.[9] Such voices, however, were outnumbered and were either ignored or engendered hostile responses. For the participants who acted to ensure that the name of the Persian Gulf remains unchanged, the specific body of water was not at the core of what was at stake. For them, the issue was about national identity and the history of Iran.

In the spaces of the Iranian Internet, sensitive issues such as this can function as litmus tests for identifying who counts as a member of the community of Iranians. In other words, while the Internet allows for this transnationally dispersed group to gather and define itself, it also provides the tools for narrowing the boundaries of who may participate and how to participate in newly created public spheres. As digital media practices and technologies develop alongside one another, so do the processes of constructing and propagating nationalisms, including those that are based on troubling appeals to gender and race.

Static Web Sites and the Rise of Web 2.0

For the remainder of the 1990s and in the early years of the millennium, Iranian.com functioned as a central hub for drawing attention to and discussing issues related to the Persian Gulf.[10] By the early 2000s, however, new online avenues had opened where the issue could be discussed. Some of these sites continued to follow Web 1.0 frameworks, but an increase in the number of blogs indicated that a transition to the interactive Web was under way. Web sites dedicated solely to the issue sprang up in this period. The turn to user-constructed Web sites was a significant development. More individuals and groups established themselves online in this decade instead of merely flocking to the few sites set up by the tech-savvy elite.

The Web site of the Persian Gulf Taskforce, a basic static site, is a good example of the latter. The site remained largely the same from the time it went online in the early 2000s. The Taskforce traced its origin to the Persian Gulf Organization, a predecessor founded in 1998. The former cites its mission as the "defense and preservation of the historic name of the Persian Gulf."[11] Although the organization's Web site claimed to have chapters worldwide, citing locations and occasionally the names of board members affiliated with a chapter, it did not provide information about the specific activities of any particular chapter.[12] The only offline location affiliated with the site was a California PO box address on the contact page of the site.[13] To the extent that it provided the names of a handful of founders and board members whose identity and activism in the Iranian Diaspora community can be confirmed with research, the organization provided some transparency about its membership. At the same time, the lack of evidence of its assertion that it had chapters worldwide raises questions about how the Internet makes it possible for one individual or a handful of people to claim that they represent broader offline communities. While an offline constituency may not be an urgent concern in the case of a single Web site such as this one, the relationship between the virtual and the offline world cannot be entirely dismissed. In fact, it

Figure 1. A screen capture taken in 2007 from the main page of the Web site of the Persian Gulf Task Force. The organization has had an online presence since at least 2001. It was formerly available at http://www.persiangulfonline. org/ and until fall of 2012 was available at http://persiangulftaskforce.org/.

becomes a central problem in other cases involving the Iranian Internet that bear more directly on local and global political developments.

The rhetoric of the Persian Gulf Taskforce site included arguments similar to those used in the 1996 mobilization and in subsequent online debates. The site identified "ultra-nationalist Arab chauvinists" as aggressors, for example, implying a contrast between Iran's "documented history" and the history of its Arab neighbors. The site claims to be nonpartisan and nonpolitical, but it places the blame for the increasing prevalence of the term "Arabian Gulf" on the Iranian state and claims that "in the absence of decisive action by the Iranian government, it is up to us to defend the heritage of Iran."[14] Although the organization expresses its goals in relatively measured tones that do not rely on the racist terms found in other responses to the Persian Gulf issue, its core arguments about the Iranian government and Arab states share similarities with accounts that come close to or completely cross the line of racist tropes.

The short-lived Web site of the Persian Gulf Defense Fund is another example of a page that cropped up during this period and was entirely dedicated to the Persian Gulf issue. The Defense Fund is another organization that was located only online and was registered in southern California while the group's Web site was active. It blamed "our old enemies" (i.e., the Arabs) as the source of the renaming of the Persian Gulf and identified itself as the "defender of the [Iranian] cultural identity" in the face of what it described as the Iranian government's failure to act in protecting Iran's "inalienable rights."[15]

Although the Web sites of the Persian Gulf Taskforce and the Persian Gulf Defense Fund clearly differ in the language they use, they both appeal to the binary of a passive government and an aggressive enemy that necessitates a decisive response. Both sites appeal to history and the historical significance of the name of the Persian Gulf and cast themselves and their supporters as defenders of Iranian territories and heritage. This general framework was also visible in the English-language Diasporic online discourses about the name for the Persian Gulf.[16]

BLURRED BOUNDARIES: CONTESTED BODIES AND THE PERSIAN GULF

The debate about the naming of the Persian Gulf and the claims about Iranian history to which that debate is linked expand into broader discussions about Iranian women and (often-feminized) Iranian territories. The blurring of the boundaries between the two is easily understood, given that both rely on gendered and racialized claims for their arguments. The discussion often focuses on three islands in the Persian Gulf: Abu Musa and the Greater and Lesser Tunbs. These were claimed for decades by both Iran and the United Arab Emirates (UAE). These disputes are frequently brought up during the Persian Gulf debates and fuel much nationalistic sentiment online.[17] Specifically, they allow for the formulation of a nationalism predicated on a racialized, masculine enemy and feminized territories that must be protected.

This link was apparent from the first successful online mobilization in 1996. One reader noted that "once they [the Arab countries] change the name and get away with it, then they can justify their claims to three islands in the area."[18] While participants such as this poster may be right to point out the connection between the importance of names and territorial claims, the ways the arguments about the significance of naming collapse into gendered and racialized constructions that seek to arouse nationalistic fervor are noteworthy. These tendencies became more clearly apparent as the arenas for and tactics of online activism expanded on the Iranian Internet. Because the themes and underpinnings of these formulations remain largely unchanged, it is helpful to provide a brief overview of their structure before moving to an examination of the next stage in the developments in Internet technologies and mobilizations related to the Persian Gulf.

Claims about the importance of naming and its broader ramifications and arguments about the motivations of states that use the term "Arabian" to describe the Persian Gulf are legitimate and are often backed with solid evidence. What is at issue here is not the merit of the core arguments but the terms of the nationalisms that are used to fuel the responses. Like all formulations of nationalisms, the pillars underpinning the arguments for why "Persian" is the only appropriate label for the body of water depend on difference. In other words, since the main point of contention is the attempt to change the name of the gulf to "Arabian," the Arabs are the "other" that stand outside the national unity.[19] This difference is usually not stated neutrally but in terms that implicitly or directly assert the superiority of Iran. Thus, as noted in the examples from static Web sites dedicated to the issue, the "Persian" label of the gulf is construed as embodying a unique history. Moreover, these debates often stress that Iran's history is "documented": that is to say, evidence for Iran's long history (and claims to the name of the gulf) can be found in books, maps, and artifacts. The problem with appeals to historical documentation, however, is that they are often paired with constructions of Arabs as savage, as being rich in oil money but not in culture or history. As a result, arguments that may otherwise have a basis in geopolitical realities—namely, that the Arab states' attempts to rename the Persian Gulf are rooted in their efforts to exercise greater control of the region—sometimes collapse into racist claims about the leaders and inhabitants of those states.

An implicit clash of masculinities is often at work in this debate. On the one side is the honorable man, the Iranian who is defending the motherland, and on the other side is the invader, the Arab who, according to many such arguments, has been making claims on Iranian land and Iranian women for over 1,400 years. In these discussions, Iranian territories and women are often conflated: rescuing Iranian land overlaps with protecting Iranian women. One can easily trace in these themes what Cynthia Enloe has called nationalism's reliance on "masculinized memory, masculinized humiliation, and masculinized hope" (Enloe 1989, 44).

The Iranian state figures prominently in many of these discussions, particularly in the discourses of those who openly or implicitly take an oppositional or critical stance toward the government. In these cases, the Iranian state appears at once emasculated and menacing: it is emasculated because it is unable to defend itself against the Arab invaders and it is menacing because it is a threat to its own people, not just because of its policies but because it is not defending the heritage and honor of Iran. The Islamic character of the current Iranian government adds a complicating layer to the racialized nature of the nationalistic discussions, as many who participate in the particularly extreme versions of this nationalism deliberately elide the distinction between Islam and Arabs, giving rise to an entire subset of discourses that compare the Iranian government to Arab occupiers who are in collusion with the country's Arab neighbors.[20] Within these nationalist mobilizations, formulations of a vulnerable and inadequately defended Persian Gulf necessitate a robust response that is often articulated in the language of militarism and vigilantism.

The following excerpts from a particularly virulent letter posted to Iranian.com reflect how many of these themes work side by side in such accounts.

> The idea of changing the Persian Gulf to aka Arabian Gulf did not develop just yesterday. However now, with an Arab friendly regime in Iran, it is much easier for the pan-Arab nationalist[s] to achieve what they wanted fifty years ago. The regime in Iran will not challenge them, and why should they? . . . For a long time [the Islamic Republic] tried to prevent us from celebrating our national customs and cultural traditions but failed. On the other hand, they also tried to bring Arab customs, language, and culture and force it on us, and so far they have succeeded. . . . Yes, we have lost our pride and identity since the Mullahs took over. They have basically sold us out to the Arabs. Our sisters are working in whore houses in Dubai and other Sheikhdoms with full knowledge of the Iranian government. . . . I consider all those who travel to any Arab country and spend money traitors to the Iranian people and the Iranian

nation. They are back stabbers to all those heroes and soldiers who gave their life to protect Iran and our nation from the Arab invasion 1400 years ago to the 1980s Iranian and Iraq war.[21]

While the Internet facilitated the creation of spaces outside the immediate purview of the state where participants could put a critical or oppositional spin on popular issues, new technologies opened the same doors for state powers to expand their field of influence. The Persian Gulf debates illustrate that the Iranian state was aware of the opportunities available through digital media and began to openly assert itself online in the era of Web 2.0.

Persian Web 2.0: New Methods for Old Arguments

The late 1990s and early 2000s were the last years when English-language sites dominated the Persian Gulf debate. Persian-language sites overtook their English-language counterparts on the Iranian Internet in the new millennium. With developments that made it easy to use Persian script and the rise of forms of self-publishing such as blogs, the terrain of the entire Iranian Internet radically changed in key ways. English rapidly lost its dominance among the Diasporic elements of the Iranian Internet, and Persian became the primary language. The development of Unicode was key in making it possible for writers to use Persian script online.[22] In addition, at the turn of the millennium, there was a spike in tech-savvy Diasporic twenty- and thirtysomethings who were fluent in Persian but were not comfortable with the language of the host country. This meant that the Diasporic elements of the Iranian Internet increasingly used Persian. In addition, the development of a Persian digital character set allowed older members of the Diaspora who may have never become proficient in any language other than Persian to have their work disseminated online.[23] Iran-based participation also rapidly increased during this period and would soon overtake both the English-speaking and Persian-speaking Diaspora on the Internet.

While technological developments played a crucial role, they are not a sufficient explanation for the shifts in the terrain of the Iranian Internet. They must be considered alongside internal and global political developments. The first successful online mobilization around the

Persian Gulf naming issue occurred at the dawn of the reformist movement, but by the early years of the new millennium, the movement was
in decline. Between 1996 and the next big moment of activism around
the Persian Gulf in 2004, Saddam Hussein and the Taliban, regional
enemies of Iran, had fallen thanks to the United States. This created
mixed responses: the Iranian government celebrated the fall of both
enemies but had to contend with the fact that it was now surrounded
by a heavy U.S. presence. Internally, political conflicts between weak-
ening reformist camps and conservative factions in Iran resulted in
the closing of many reformist publications, and a significant number
of the journalists and political activists associated with the movement
began to populate the Internet as an alternate site of expression and
activism. This turn to the Internet, including the rapidly proliferat-
ing Persian-language blogosphere, became the subject of widespread
attention, including in accounts produced by journalists and nongovernmental organizations in the United States and Europe. One reason
for the intense focus on the Iranian blogosphere was the government's
persecution of several journalists turned bloggers.[24] Restrictions on
publishing both on and off line resulted in the emigration of a significant number of well-known writers and supporters of reformist
publications.

In short, Iran's highly factionalized internal power struggles played
a key—albeit inconsistent and difficult-to-discern—role in shaping
the state of Iranian politics and the online spaces to which it is linked.
By 2004, when the next moment of heightened activity occurred in the
Persian Gulf debates, major changes had occurred in Internet technology, the internal situation in Iran, the Iranian Diaspora, and the general world political context. This moment of intense mobilization was
precipitated by the publication of the eighth edition of the *National
Geographic Society Atlas of the World*, which included the term "Arabian Gulf" in parentheses near the name Persian Gulf, prompting one
of the largest responses on the Iranian Internet to date.

In earlier periods, the Internet was mainly used as a vehicle for
attracting attention to the cause, writing and distributing arguments
in favor of action, and submitting grievances and e-mails online. Participants used the capacities provided by new technologies to the full
extent available at the time. The responses to the National Geographic

publication showed a notable turn to existing Web sites and forums such as those provided by Iranian.com to write letters, offer analyses, and share tactics about what could and had been done. Compared to the 1996 incident involving in-flight maps provided by the KLM airline and other issues involving the Persian Gulf in the early years of the millennium, the scale of the response to the National Geographic publication is remarkable. While some of this reflects the importance granted to the National Geographic Society as an institution that names and designates geographical entities, the shift in the scale of responses is also linked to the growth of the Iranian Internet, which by then had expanded in terms of the number and diversity of Iranians online and offered a greater number of virtual locations. Most important, participants had begun to tinker with existing technologies in order to maximize their efforts.

The best example of an innovative approach in this period is seen in the creation of a Google bomb that came to play a central role in the online mobilizations during this period. An Iranian blogger in Canada created a Google bomb for the term "Arabian Gulf" by designing a webpage with the URL http://arabian-gulf.info/. He then encouraged others to create links to it on their Web sites using the label "Arabian Gulf" and to click on those links repeatedly. The idea was to exploit the algorithm Google's search engine used at that time. The algorithm identified the relationship between certain search terms and specific URLs and increased the rank of a particular page according to the number of times a particular search term was linked to it.

This idea spread on the blogosphere and on scores of other Web sites, and enough people clicked on the URL to influence the results. When anyone searched the Internet using the term "Arabian Gulf," the page designed by the Google bomber would be among the top results. Enough participants heeded the call to link to and/or click on the URL that the page reached the first spot in a Google search and remained there for many years. The URL took readers to what looked like an error page with the following message: "The Gulf you are looking for does not exist. Try Persian Gulf. The gulf you are looking for is unavailable. No body of water by that name has ever existed. The correct name is Persian Gulf, which always has been, and will always remain, Persian." In addition to the hundreds of blogs and Web sites of

← → 🌐 http://arabian-gulf.info/   🔍 ▾ 🔖 ⭕ ✕ 🌐 Arabian Gulf   ✕

ℹ **The Gulf You Are Looking For Does Not Exist. Try** Persian Gulf.

The gulf you are looking for is unavailable. No body of water by that name has ever existed. The correct name is Persian Gulf, which always has been, and will always remain, Persian.

Please try the following:

- Click the 🗗 button, and never try again.
- If you typed Arabian Gulf, make sure you read some history books.
- Click 🔍 Search to look for more information on the internet.

TRUTH 404- Gulf Not Found
Fact Explorer

What is this page? Click to find out

Figure 2. The most successful of the Persian Gulf Google bomb campaigns was designed by Iranian artist and blogger Pendar Yousefi. In 2013, this page was still among the top results that appeared when the search term "Arabian Gulf" is used, although the site is no longer available.

individuals and organizations who participated in making the Google bomb reach its goal, others contributed with the construction of new pages that could also be "bombed."[25]

Another Web-based mode of action that was new to this period was the use of an online petition that targeted the National Geographic Society. Although the petition—online or otherwise—is a mundane and hackneyed form of activism, this one obtained over 100,000 signatures, an unprecedented number for any previous petition drafted by or about Iranians.[26]

In short, this period reflects a marked change from dependence on written texts and static Web sites to a broader use of Web sites, blogs, and user-generated content that went beyond merely writing to manipulating search engine algorithms and even using animation and video.[27]

While the responses to the Persian Gulf issue clearly grew in tandem with the growth of technologies, the terms of the discourse were largely static. Participants continued to walk a fine line between political analysis that accused Arab petrodollars of financing the name change and racist tropes of menacing Arabs. Discussions about the relationship between naming and claims over territory, including the three disputed islands, similarly slid into gendered, if not racialized, assertions. Although the issue of Iranian women's prostitution was no longer as prominent as it had been in earlier periods, it still cropped up occasionally in the course of discussions that sought to stir nationalistic outrage over the name change.[28] And racialized and gendered strands were often central to the accounts that linked the Persian Gulf issue to criticism of the Iranian government, at once portraying the state as a hypermasculine aggressive threat to its neighbors and people and an insufficiently masculine servant of Arab interests.

These tendencies were particularly evident in the case of the online petition drafted in response to the publication of the *National Geographic Atlas of the World*. Addressing itself to the National Geographic Society, the petition insisted that the "Persian Gulf is a genuine name, with historical roots" and that referring to the body of water by any other name or labeling the three islands as occupied by Iran was not acceptable. The petition also claimed that the National Geographic's actions in this regard were politically motivated and had "hurt the national pride of the millions of Persian speakers."[29] Some of those who signed the petition chose to leave comments alongside their names, and many comments reiterated the points about the influence of oil money, that the National Geographic was attempting to rewrite history, and that Iranians would stand in the way of any such changes. While a notable number of signers who commented explicitly distanced themselves from racist sentiments, the anonymous public space allowed others to comfortably express virulent anti-Arab ideas, many of which showed the tendency to conflate present-day Arabs with the historical Arabs who were responsible for the attacks on the Persian Empire. Other signers directly implicated the Iranian state; some listed details of Iran's internal and foreign policies, while others resorted to accusations that blurred the lines between Islam, Arabs, and the current Iranian government. Like most online versions, the petition did not provide a way of verifying the identity of the signatories, leaving the door open for multiple signatures under assumed names and other forms of duplicity.

Although the state was a target of many during this period, it took an active role in response to the Persian Gulf issue and capitalized on the opportunities the convergence of the offline and the virtual provided.

NEW MEDIA STATE

In the earliest years of online activism around the issue of the name for the Persian Gulf, the narrative of an emasculated state that pandered to Arab invaders could appear to hold some merit. The borders of the Iranian Internet were much narrower and were the dominion of the Diaspora, who are more likely to be critical of—if not opposed to— the Iranian state.[30] More important, the state seemed to play no significant role online; any offline action it may have taken was virtually invisible. In 2004, however, it became clear that the state recognized the importance of using the Internet. The participation of the state in the Persian Gulf debates is also noteworthy because it shows how the Internet can be used to magnify steps that have been taken offline. Those who have the means of carrying out massive action offline and/ or have access to other forms of media have an advantage; they are able to benefit from the convergence of a greater number of arenas.

During the 2004 mobilizations around the issue of the name of the Persian Gulf, the state seemed to take advantage of all of its options. In addition to delivering a formal protest to the National Geographic Society, the Iranian government banned the sale of the Society's publications in Iran and withdrew an invitation previously given to a *National Geographic* photo editor who had been asked to participate in a conference. They took similar action against the Al-Jazeera network for its dissemination of a cartoon poking fun at the government's concern over the name of the Persian Gulf.[31] Special issues of popular daily newspapers, such as Tehran municipality's high-circulation paper *Hamshahri*, were dedicated to stirring national sentiment and arguing against the dual naming of the gulf.

These offline activities were supplemented and expanded online through a number of channels. Official Web sites were launched in support of the government's efforts, and political figures in Iran used their blogs and Web sites to express solidarity with campaigns against changing the name of the Persian Gulf. For example, Mohammad Ali

Figure 3. The November 16, 2004, blog post of Mohammad Ali Abtahi, who at the time was vice-president of Iran, in support of Persian Gulf campaigns. Abtahi, a reformist, was a pioneer in embracing digital media and was the first official to start a personal blog.

Abtahi, who was vice-president of Iran at the time, used his personal blog as a vehicle for supporting state and individual efforts to challenge the National Geographic Society. He also proudly credited blogging Iranians as being in the vanguard of activism on the issue.[32]

On a larger scale, the Ministry of Culture and Islamic Guidance launched the Internet-based Persian Gulf Festival on a Web site that stood out in terms of the technology and rhetoric it used. The home page of the site featured a prominent link to the Diaspora-generated online petition, proudly labeling it the "biggest online Iranian protest,"[33] a fact that is particularly noteworthy, considering that many signers of the petition used the comments feature to malign the government. In contrast to the largely static Web sites that had sprung up over the years in defense of the Persian Gulf, the ministry-generated site reflected a convergence of old and new media. The site included a contest as part of the festival that called for online submissions in a variety of formats, including best animation, best short story, and best blog on the theme of "The Eternally Persian Gulf," a phrase that by then was familiar from the early days of the discourse on the issue.[34] Winning submissions reproduced almost word for word the claims found in Diasporic discourse despite the fact that much of the latter articulates a nationalism that is opposed to the current government. Winning submissions, for example, glorified the "bravery of men" who had loved and protected the Persian Gulf,[35] used racist images to accuse the Gulf Arabs of financing the name change in an attempt to erase Iranian history,[36] and celebrated the role of the Internet in mobilizing people against the perceived enemy.[37]

Thus, not only did the state step openly into the online landscape to magnify its actions offline and to open an entirely new front in its propaganda efforts, it also easily co-opted the work of nonstate actors and individuals, including those who opposed it. Like the efforts of some nonstate actors, official provocation of nationalistic sentiments depended on appeals to history, depictions of aggressive enemies lusting for Iranian territories, and the language of defense in the face of invaders. The Iranian state's open and multilayered participation on the Internet clearly shows that understanding the relationship between the government and digital media necessitates going beyond accounts that focus on the state's attempts to monitor or restrict online activities.

CONCLUSION

From the late 1990s to the early years of the new millennium, major changes took place in terms of the technologies available, the populations participating, and the ways that new tools were used on the Iranian Internet. Attempts to change the name of the Persian Gulf consistently rile Iranians from a variety of geographical and ideological backgrounds, and the debates around the issue provide a particularly useful case study for tracing how advances in the technology unfolded in tandem with changes in the makeup of the Iranian Internet as well as how the technologies were used. The interlinked developments in the Persian Gulf mobilizations and the Iranian Internet also show how digital spheres, far from being a hindrance to the propagation of nationalisms, are compatible with it. While Internet technologies facilitate the gathering of disparately located individuals, it is nationalism that in some sense does the heavy lifting in motivating and maintaining the transnational mobilizations that digital media makes possible.

Similarly noteworthy are the terms of the nationalisms used in the discourse of the Internet-enhanced activism around the Persian Gulf.

The consequences of choosing a name are by no means neutral, and when important geographical entities such as the Persian Gulf are involved, any name change will have political and cultural implications. The terms with which the concerns of users of the Iranian Internet were expressed, particularly by Diasporic populations seeking to reassert their ties to the homeland, were very troubling.

Finally, the Persian Gulf case study highlights how the Internet provided an opportunity for the state to magnify its activities offline and open new arenas for action online, in the process absorbing and co-opting even the efforts of those who were critical of the government. The Iranian state proved itself to be as dynamic and crafty in its approach to digital media as its nonstate counterparts.

The state's participation in the Persian Gulf issue is only the beginning of how it took up digital media in the new millennium. Discourses about the Iranian Internet of this era often focus on sites that are critical of or oppose the ruling structure. But the state and its supporters—whether those supporters are sponsored by official government entities or act on their own—also took to the blogosphere in this period. Chapter 2 examines the rise of the Iranian blogosphere in all of its diversity and contradictions.

CHAPTER 2

UNCHARTED
BLOGOSPHERES

The Iranian blogosphere, one of the most vibrant components of the Iranian Internet, presents a rich and varied landscape that traverses ideological and geographic boundaries. Iranians' early and enthusiastic embrace of blogging inspired excitement among Iran and media scholars, journalists, and human rights and other civil society organizations. Although the discourse among Weblogistan enthusiasts largely focused on its oppositional aspects (where the concept of opposition was often equated with secular or anti-religious/anti-Islam voices), such discourses have also made a solid case that the blogosphere was well suited for expressions of dissent and challenges to the interpretations of past and present events that ruling power structures favor and as an alternate route of disseminating information. While these aspects of Weblogistan continue to garner attention, large swaths of its territory remains unexamined.

Furthermore, while the Internet is primarily the domain of nonstate actors, the state's hand is not absent in participating in and influencing the blogosphere, particularly in matters that touch on issues central to its vision of itself. However, analysis of Weblogistan and the Iranian Internet in general tend to consider the state in two interrelated ways: as a singular entity that represses bloggers or as a singular entity that bloggers rebel against, both of which do reflect major functions of the Iranian state vis-à-vis the blogosphere. Yet this framework captures only a part of the state's complex and conflicted relationship to Weblogistan, since it also devotes significant resources to shaping discourses on and about the blogosphere.

Focusing on the period roughly covering 2003–2008, when blog-ging was at its height, this chapter provides a supplement to exist-ing narratives about Weblogistan from two complementary angles. First, it examines examples from distinct but overlapping catego-ries of blogs that are often either entirely overlooked or are only briefly considered in the dominant literature about Weblogistan. In their own ways belying a number of misconceptions about Iran and the blogosphere, these blogs also reflect serious fissures in Iranian society and the political structure. Although they may not take up issues from the secular or oppositional perspectives favored by many mainstream accounts of Weblogistan, these bloggers do not shrink from using the medium in ways that challenge social and political mores. Second, this chapter considers a number of state-sponsored actions aimed at shaping and using Weblogistan. The actions the government took to suppress the blogosphere, such as filtering con-tent, blocking access, and in some cases arresting bloggers, show that the ruling system is aware of the serious challenge Weblogistan may pose. But some actions the state took reveal that it also appre-ciates the opportunities the blogosphere presents for promoting its cultural and political agendas. The steps that state actors took in this regard represent a significant development in its stance toward Weblogistan; clearly it is perceived as a space where both coercive and diffuse forms of power can be exercised.

Maps of Weblogistan: Well-Trodden and Hidden Territory

Few aspects of the Iranian Internet have been more widely cele-brated than the blogosphere. Weblogistan, which was at its prime from late 2002 to 2008, has been the subject of scores of popular and scholarly accounts, most of which emphasize its oppositional and liberatory goals. Such characterizations of the Iranian blogo-sphere generally take two overlapping forms. Drawing on several high-profile instances of the government's persecution of bloggers, one set of accounts identifies the blogosphere as primarily a political and politicized space (Bucar and Fazaeli 2008; Rahimi 2003). Other accounts highlight how Weblogistan broke taboos. Such accounts often mention how blogs provided a liberating space for women

(Alavi 2005; Amir-Ebrahimi 2008b). Whether their focus is on the social or political aspects of Weblogistan, these analysts usually emphasize how bloggers push against the state. The nongovernmental[1] and think tank sectors have played a key role as knowledge producers about the Iranian Internet and its blogosphere in particular. Although such accounts underline the repressive measures of the state, they also emphasize the potential of digital media, especially blogging, to circumvent restrictions and create conditions for democratic change.[2]

To be sure, the government's repressive measures, in particular those directed at online spheres, are important for understanding the development of the Iranian Internet. All bloggers writing from Iran, regardless of genre or political persuasion, at some point will have to get around blocked access to content.[3] And although the well-publicized accounts of persecuted bloggers did not prevent Weblogistan from thriving and expanding, they likely played a role in the decisions of at least some bloggers to protect their identities and to go to great pains to remain anonymous online. In addition, the blogosphere's role in opening avenues for pushing social boundaries cannot be discounted, nor is it unique to Iran. However, reading Weblogistan primarily through this lens overshadows the richness of its landscape, in some cases providing skewed assessments that exaggerate the extent to which security concerns and resisting the ruling power structure dominate the blogosphere.

Several works have stepped outside the strict confines of these models, providing revealing glimpses into largely unexamined territory. Alireza Doostdar's 2004 study offers a linguistic analysis of blogging as a new kind of speech genre and highlights how Weblogistan created opportunities for intellectual confrontations among those with disparate access to cultural capital. Annabelle Sreberny and Gholam Khiabany (2007) have gone beyond a focus on sensationalized bloggers to highlight Weblogistan as an arena of diverse intellectual production. They have also critiqued accounts that draw a monolithic portrait of the Iranian blogosphere, instead calling for frameworks that understand digital media in relation to previous and existing policies, technologies, and political dynamics (Sreberny and Khiabany 2011). Others have critiqued the liberation model, pointing out that narrowly conceived narratives can be exclusionary: focusing only on secular or anti-state forms of resistance, they leave out other forms of challenging social and political systems (Akhavan 2011). Others argue that far from breaking free from gender-based constraints, bloggers are subject to gendered discourses of militarism and neoliberalism (Shakshari 2011). While Masserat Amir-Ebrahimi's work on gender on the blogosphere has repeated some of the claims about its liberatory powers, her work on religious Iranians online casts light on often-ignored segments of Weblogistan. Her work considers blogging and other Internet practices of seminary students, showing that their engagement is not confined to the officially promoted activity of propagating state-sanctioned ideas about Islam (Amir-Ebrahimi 2008a).

Even in policy-oriented publications—a body of work that has largely followed the model of Weblogistan as one that is almost exclusively dominated by oppositional writers—at least one observer has argued that it is important to pay attention to the large numbers of bloggers who do not fit this mold and who offer policy makers a more accurate sense of the Iranian public's views on key topics, including the nuclear issue (Pedatzur 2008). Similarly, in an interdisciplinary study combining human and automated content analysis, researchers at the Berkman Center for Internet and Society concluded that "the early conventional wisdom that Iranian bloggers are mainly young democrats critical of the regime" contrasted with their own findings that the Iranian blogosphere is diverse in terms of political opinions and topics covered (Kelly and Etling 2008, 24). This small but compelling body of work indicates that there is much unexplored terrain in the transnational blogosphere that reveals the complexities of contemporary Iran and Weblogistan itself.

For entirely different reasons, the Iranian state has also fought to challenge the prevailing portrayal of Weblogistan as primarily oppositional and/or secular. The Ministry of Culture and Guidance took an interest in examining the blogosophere, and in 2006, it published the first of a multiyear series of studies about Weblogistan. This study and a range of proposals by the ministry and other governmental institutions or affiliates (discussed below) are an indication of the state's acute interest and active investment in using the blogosphere as a site of cultural and political production.

Case Studies from Outside the Fold

One assumption about bloggers who are identified (or misidentified) as being close to the hardline elements of the ruling system is that they operate online as agents executing explicit orders. It is indeed true that there are those who openly operate in the interest of particular political agendas.[4] These blogs are fairly easy to recognize, as they tend to be impersonal and monolithic in the topics they discuss and the stances they take. Yet most bloggers who fall outside the framework favored by popular accounts produced by Diasporics and journalists outside Iran tend to cover topics that range from personal anecdotes to daily observations about society and politics to debates about historic or contemporary controversies. At the most basic level, a consideration of these blogs complicates and demystifies often-repeated categorizations of Iranian youth as politically and sexually rebellious (in a context where the mere fact of sexual activity is read as a political act against the government).[5] The blogs considered below demonstrate the social and political realities bloggers tackle and the contexts out of which they arise. The content some bloggers publish tracks significant changes in their personal or political outlook, hinting at broader societal shifts and providing insight into the factors that precipitate such change.

Zahra HB is an example of a blogger who was not included in celebratory accounts of Weblogistan because of her social and political conservatism. However, her prolific blogging output since 2002 and her vast readership make her impossible to ignore.[6] Much of the attention she received has been scornful, especially from fellow Netizens participating in debates about the blogosphere. These interblog battles over Zahra HB, whose site is one of the few that provides links to those from diverse political backgrounds and geographical locales, are noteworthy for what they show about the limits of the blogosphere as a new space for open dialogue. But aside from the meta-discourses her writings have engendered on the blogosphere, the site itself is important for what it reveals about the nuances of daily life, politics, and blogging in Iran.

For example, Zahra HB regularly writes about what she experiences on various forms of transit, often including an analysis of contemporary society and politics in her observations. In a January 2007 post, she recounted a conversation she had heard earlier in the day in a taxi: a heavily made up teenage girl "sitting in the lap" of a young man called her sister, instructing her to tell their mother that she had been at a girlfriend's home (instead of with her boyfriend) and asking her to bring her a wet rag (to wipe off her makeup) and her chador (a conservative form of customary *hejab* in Iran).[7] At first glance, there is nothing remarkable about the story of a teenager sneaking around and quickly wiping off her makeup and changing her clothes before returning home to deliver a story about having spent the day studying with a friend. Indeed, the structure of the story fits very well with narratives about Iranian youth in general that emphasizes the ways this generation is defying a restrictive state, a process that forces Iranians to have contradictory interior and exterior lives.[8] Yet the story here is about family restrictions, not state restrictions. Nor is this an account about the youth from secular backgrounds whose stories are often privileged in mainstream accounts. Finally, the observation does not come from a source who considers herself outside of or hostile to the kind of traditional family she describes. In short, what seems like an ordinary tale of youthful defiance takes on other layers of significance when one considers the details of the story and the point of view from which it is narrated.

Many of the readers who responded to the post in the comments section shared similar situations they had witnessed, often criticizing the family. Such exchanges not only reveal potential generational rifts in contemporary Iranian society, they also show that such tensions cannot be fully explained using frameworks that understand social limitations primarily through the lens of the Iranian state, no matter how forceful that state may be in attempting to impose its version of proper behavior.

Zahra HB's blog contains dozens of posts tagged with labels such as "taxi," "bus," "metro," each of which provide the writer's thoughts and observations as she traverses back and forth across the city. Covering everything from the singers most favored by taxi drivers to public transportation etiquette to friendly and humorous exchanges among passengers, these posts tend to have a lighthearted tone. In fact, the overall feel of Zahra HB's site is cheerful; its template is a pink background filled with roses, her logo is a picture of a doll, and her posts are written in a diary-like manner. Yet she does not shy away from taking up serious issues and registering her objections to the policies or discourses she disagrees with. In 2007, she criticized a proposed government plan for regulating strict adherence to the Islamic dress code. She referred to a picture taken by a reformist journalist of a young girl pleading with the police not to detain her mother for dress code violations:

> Although I believe in *hejab*, never and under no circumstances could I hurt someone physically or mentally (and to this degree) over something like [the dress code] or anything else. Does that mean that my faith is weak? Or that their way is the right way? Do you really think this is the way to enact *amr-e be maroof* [the Islamic imperative that Muslims are to guide other Muslims] or to prevent corruption? It is strange to me that some of the police are women. Does their work make them impervious to the cries and the begging of girls and women or is that how they were before? I would really like to hear the views of those who agree with regulating dress codes in accordance to this current method. It might be interesting for you to know that at

Figure 4. An April 2007 post from the blog Zahra criticizing methods police forces used to enforce dress codes for Iranian women.

lunch today I was discussing the matter with some of my co-workers [who strictly follow Islamic dress codes] and they were all against this way and I really haven't seen anyone who agrees.[9]

The enforcement of an Islamic dress code is a clear example of the state's imposition of its interpretation of moral tenets on the populace, and it is widely commented upon and criticized on the blogosphere and offline. If one focuses only on secular responses to the actions of a state with fundamental theocratic components, it is easy to infer that religious bloggers either do not exist in significant numbers or that they are mindlessly supportive of government actions. The presence of bloggers such as Zahra HB belies these notions, once again underlining the importance of uncovering the complexities of the state, society, and the blogosphere in Iran.

While much of what Zahra HB comments on relates to her lived experience and her observations about the local manifestations of national policies, she situates her blogging self transnationally and regularly discusses developments outside Iran. The range of issues she covers is broad. For example, she expressed sorrow about the Virginia Tech shootings of April 2007 but noted that Iranians should be grateful that the perpetrator was not a Muslim or the incident would have given rise to more anti-Muslim sentiments. In support of the latter point, she quoted an Iranian blogger living in the United States.[10] She also discusses regional issues; many posts are about Israel, Palestine, and Iraq.[11] As almost all of her entries address a number of disparate issues, even the most serious topics are often considered alongside recollections of daily events. As a consequence, the blog does not come across as polemical but instead gives the impression that the reader is gaining access to Zahra HB's thoughts on all manner of topics.

In contrast, Bahman Hedayati's site creates no illusion of a comfortable, familiar space. This is clearly indicated by its name, Digital Kalashnikov. The blog's title refers to Hedayati's work as a photographer and journalist, but it also characterizes the tone of his posts. In his inaugural post in 2003, he explicitly talked about blogs as instruments of cultural and political warfare.[12] Identifying with the Principalist camp in Iranian politics (a conservative faction that is aligned with centers of power in the ruling system and became well known after the first election of Mahmoud Ahmadinejad),[13] Hedayati devotes many blog posts

Figure 5. An October 2008 post on the blog Digital Kalashnikov, featuring a photo of the author, Bahman Hedayati, approaching Ayatollah Rafsanjani for an interview. The blog contains many posts that are harshly critical of Rafsanjani and his political allies.

to critiquing reformists and other political rivals. Numerous entries are dedicated to sarcastic and vitriolic critiques of Ayatollah Rafsanjani, a former president and a powerful member of the establishment who is not strictly self-identified as a reformist but who has increasingly aligned with them during Ahmadinejad's presidential terms.[14] In addition to taking aim at powerful figures from opposing political factions, the site also includes more general—and less hostile—criticism of the clergy and people of faith for their involvement in politics, claiming in one post that their entrenchment in politics has created distance between them and the problems of ordinary people.[15] In a country where the ruling system is based on the embeddedness of the clergy in the power structure, Hedayati's claim is a bold one, especially considering his expressed loyalty to the government.

Hedayati's posts are routinely devoted to the specificities of Iran's internal politics, and it seems reasonable to assume that his intended readers are Iran-based bloggers and readers. But a broader audience is involved, as indicated by the author's opening post from 2004: "Greetings to my dear friends from all around the world, (especially to the brothers and sisters in England, who, after those from Islamic Iran, make up the biggest portion of the readers of this humble virtual cottage)."[16] This awareness of an international audience may explain why he occasionally posts in both English and Persian.[17] The site also reflects both an understanding and a critique of transnational discourses about the Iranian blogosphere. In July 2003, Hedayati wrote about the arrest of his friend Soheil Karimi, a photographer and documentary filmmaker who was detained with a colleague in Iraq by American forces. The short post is mostly devoted to Hedayati's memories of Soheil and his personality, but it begins with a sharp admonition to his readers: "Soheil wasn't a blogger or into blogs. He wasn't part of the virtual world at all. So if you don't get that, if you don't know Soheil, if only the fate of the likes of Sina Motallebi is important to you, then please get out of here. Soheil has been detained by the Americans! In Iraq!"[18]

The person Hedayati mentions, Sina Motallebi, was the first blogger arrested by the Iranian government in April 2003. Like several other bloggers arrested in the subsequent year, Motallebi was a former journalist with reformist newspapers who had turned to the Internet after the government banned his publication. The case received international attention and became a hallmark of accounts that see Weblogistan as an arena where bloggers face off against a government that responds by persecuting them. Hedayati's bitter comment seems to call out the hypocrisy among those whose attention to detainees is determined by the identity of the person arrested. Whether this is a fair assessment or not, the critique of an audience accused of placing differential value on the lives of detainees indicates an understanding of the impact of the transnational web in promoting human rights issues, especially when a case involves a Netizen.[19]

Hedayati's pointed comment also reflects an ambiguity about the blogosphere and cyberspheres more broadly, as he implies that the lack of attention Soheil's case received online is at least in part due to his not "being part of the virtual world at all." In this sense his post is admonishing bloggers for a solipsism that weighs the importance of events in terms of their connections to the blogosphere. In fact, Hedayati's misgivings about blogs and the meta-discourses of the blogosphere go back to his earliest posts, which coincide with Weblogistan's boom. In March 2003, noting that the past six months had witnessed both the delirious reception of blogs and the rapid multiplication of new sites and a sudden stagnation during which many bloggers claimed they had run out of things to say, Hedayati suggested: "But it would behoove us to consider why this has happened. Why has this absolute freedom without censorship and oversight turned into a motionless, odorous pool of dead water (with a few exceptions)? Where was the problem? Why did we finish all we had to say in six months or less? What else do we have to say? What have we gained and lost in this past year? What was the cost of our presence [here]? Isn't it the case that blogs or even all manifestations of the new world have a fanciful nature for us? A fancifulness that is now boring too!"[20]

Hedayati saw the early stagnation of the blogosphere as an indisputable rebuttal of the view that Weblogistan was a free-speech utopia where Iranians could bloom outside the grip of the repressive state. In his view, blogging technologies had been embraced too quickly without adequate consideration of them as new forms of media. Despite this criticism and the slump in the blogosphere, Hedayati remained a regular blogger and Weblogistan continued to figure centrally on the Iranian Internet until the rise of social media began to edge it out in late 2007.

Although both fall into the category of blogs sidelined from celebratory accounts of the blogosphere, Zahra HB's blog and Bahman Hedayati's Digital Kalashnikov are quite distinct in style, tone, and frequency of posts. Zahra is a much more dedicated blogger who offers regular and lengthy entries, most of which recount her daily experiences, creating an intimate relationship with the reader. Hedayati's Digital Kalashnikov, on the other hand, is harsher in tone, often giving the impression that he is berating his audience. Explicitly identifying himself with the Principalist faction and regularly writing about partisan politics, Hedayati leaves no doubt about his political orientation. Zahra HB, on the other hand, does not take any dogmatic stances but is often cast in that role because of her socially conservative views.

Donya Rah Rah (Striped World), the blog of a seminary student named Kowsar, falls somewhere in between the two. Kowsar openly identifies with Principalist factions, but she is not polemical or sharp in her writing style. When she began blogging in 2002, Kowsar wrote about herself and her memories, but she decided to abandon her first site and to adopt a less personal style four years later. Surprisingly, the decision came as her first site was gaining a bigger audience and was being read by those who knew her offline.[21] Despite this change in format and tone, Donya Rah Rahi has not been stripped of all personal dimensions, and many entries are given tags such as "nostalgia," "quotidian," and "random thoughts."[22] In addition, Kowsar has divided her blogging self over several sites. The blog Sok Sok is reserved for her minimalist and experimental writings, and Gol Dokhtar is a joint blog for her and several other female seminary students.[23]

Kowsar's blog is not likely to interest those who want to discuss Weblogistan as a secular and oppositional arena. Her position as a female seminary student likely makes her case somewhat puzzling as well. It is one thing to express politically and socially conservative views as a woman from a religious background, but it is quite another to actively engage theological questions and other issues pertaining to religion as an expert in training at a seminary in the holy city of Qom, the traditional center of religious power and authority in Iran. Kowsar's discussions about religion, study, and life in Qom are not limited to her own immediate experiences but include bold observations about male seminary students and the life of the clergy. In a punchy March 2010 post entitled "Would you marry a cleric?" she considers why some religious women respond to the question with a screeching "no":

> Most of those who say "no" don't have a problem with the clergy per se, but with their clothes. And then it is not they who have a problem with the clothes, it's the problem that society has with it. Well, it's hard to be the partner of someone who can't be comfortably present in society because of what people think of him due to his clothes. There are some who will hurl insults, and then there are some who so fanatically think the clothes to be so sacred that, as some friends were saying, they even disapprove of a cleric eating a sandwich in a shop. . . . Let me say without beating around the bush, a great number say a strong "no" because of financial issues. Many seminarians are not in a good financial situation because they are studying. . . . Since I became a student in Qom last year, I realized that we hardly know anything about the life of seminary students, thanks to the cultural institutions of the country that have not forsaken any efforts in keeping the life of seminarians shrouded in mystery."[24]

Figure 6. A screen capture of "Would You Marry a Cleric?," one of the most frequently read posts on the blog of female seminary student Kowsar. The March 13, 2010, post considers the responses of religious women to the question.

Kowsar's post seems to distribute the blame for the difficulties clerics face equally between those who are extremely hostile to clerics and those who hold them in excessively high regard. Thus, while the overall sense of the post is that she is sympathetic to the latter camp, she clearly distances herself from them. Perhaps more important than her positionality is the sharp split in society the post indicates. She is a supporter of the religiously rooted ruling system, but she does not downplay the negative reception clerics may receive. This is despite the fact that the discussion may open a space to blame the government for people's discomfort with clerics. (Indeed, popular discourses about Iran produced by foreign journalists, the Diaspora, and/or the Iranian opposition, including anecdotes on the Iranian Internet, include many claims about a decline in religiosity and/or outright hostility to Islam that blames the rule of the Islamic Republic.) Many of the 200 comments Kowsar's post triggered expressed hostility toward clerics, and a number of contributors expressed anger that seminarians receive stipends while ordinary university students do not. A range of commenters were partial to seminarians, including the wife of a cleric who confirmed details of Kowsar's post by giving examples from her own life. Others came to the defense of clerics. One commenter provided a religious justification for their importance and another claimed that they have had a historical role in fighting injustice in

Iran. The comments section confirmed the split in society that Kowsar asserted in the body of the post.

Zahra HB and Bahman Hedayati explicitly locate themselves in relation to a transnational audience. Kowsar writes from the secluded center of religious study but often critically considers seminary life in order to engage with a broader audience outside her familiar settings. Despite their differences in positionality, all three bloggers cover material that ranges from personal anecdotes to sharp observations about contemporary Iran. These blogs exhibit the features that are often lauded in celebratory accounts of the Iranian Internet, and yet these sites and others like them fall outside the frameworks usually used to assess the Iranian blogosphere. Overlooking such sites results in skewed perspectives about Weblogistan. To treat such blogs as outliers is to overlook the diversity of and contradictions in contemporary Iran.

Perhaps the tendency to ignore or grudgingly acknowledge (but loudly condemn) such blogs stems from the concern that to do otherwise would indicate approval of these sites. But asserting the importance of blogs such as these in no way entails an endorsement of the social or political sensibilities they reflect. Furthermore, assessing Weblogistan—and by extension, contemporary Iranian society—in terms that privilege narrow ideas about what constitutes opposition misses many critical voices. The three bloggers examined above are very different in style, content, tone, and location but would likely be cast in a single, unexamined category if dominant frameworks for understanding the blogosphere are applied. Such approaches are also likely to miss the full spectrum of the ways the state uses digital media as a means of enhancing its power.

THE STATE OF WEBLOGISTAN

Weblogistan experienced crucial transitional moments in 2003 and 2004. Its rapid expansion attracted the attention of both international media outlets and the Iranian state, both of which recognized the political implications of the blogosphere. For the former, Weblogistan offered the prospect of confirming ideas about a repressive Iranian state that was being challenged by ordinary Iranians' access to new technologies. It had the potential to give critics of the state an opportunity to disrupt power dynamics that had long favored hard-line elements in the ruling system. The targeting of bloggers affiliated with the reform movement, including the high-profile arrest of Sina Motallebi, only confirmed the views of the Iranian state's domestic and international critics. This ensured that the government's restrictive approach to Weblogistan and digital spaces more broadly dominated accounts of the Iranian Internet. Yet repressive tactics constitute only one prong of the state's approach, and 2003–2004 marked major developments in its attempts to widen the scope of its activities.

The state's proactive—and in some instances co-optive—moves are discernible behind its more easily identified oppressive maneuvers. From the earliest years of a flourishing Weblogistan, official projects sought to influence discourses around the blogosphere and promote national narratives about Iranian history and society. On the fifteenth anniversary of Ayatollah Khomeini's death in June 2004, for example, the National Organization for Youth (a state entity) sponsored a blogging competition on the theme of "Imam [Khomeini] and Youth," awarding prizes of gold coins for the top five blogs.[25] The competition ran from the date of Khomeini's passing until the date of his birthday, August 7. Categories for entries included "The Imam in Your Own Words," "Your Memories," "Open Forum," "Commemorating the Imam," and "Students and the Imam."[26] The competition was held the next year with an expanded list of themes.[27]

Targeting an age group that likely did not have many living memories of Ayatollah Khomeini's passing—much less of his lifetime—the state-sponsored competition seemed to steer young people's engagement with blogs in a direction that linked the past and the present in an attempt to make the Islamic Republic's founding leader relevant to the new media moment. Indeed, the state has found a way for youth to be active in the process of memory making about the place and legacy of the late Ayatollah Khomeini. Rather than relying only on the wide array of instruments already at its disposal (its monopoly over broadcasting, the education system, state-owned publishing houses, publicly funded murals and posters, etc.), state organs have also mobilized participatory culture—at times gently nudging and at other times pushing—in directions that fit with its vision of itself. The National Organization for Youth's blogging competition provided a

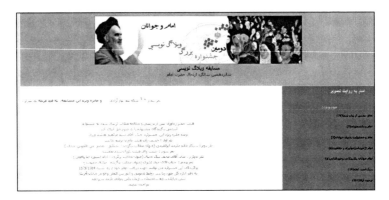

Figure 7. Announcements of the names of winners and the prizes they received
on the Web site of the Imam Khomeini and Youth blogging competition.

convenient way for the ruling powers to vicariously reassert the contemporary relevance of the Islamic Republic's founder through the
virtual mouths of its young people.

   Although prizes provided incentives to participate, the blogging
competition clearly targeted young people who were already supporters of the ruling system. In other words, while it may have been successful in further entrenching the importance of Ayatollah Khomeini
to those who constitute the base of support for the government, the
blogging competition was unlikely to stir the sentiments of disaffected
youth. For this reason, state powers cast wider nets in order to draw
the participation of bigger swaths of Iranian society by appealing to
nationalistic sentiments.

   Given the highly factional nature of the Iranian state and the
challenges it faces from both internal opposition and opposition
from members of the Diaspora, what defines the Iranian nation and
national identity are highly contested issues. Yet a few topics manage
to transcend fissures and draw the nationalistic ire of broad segments
of resident and Diaspora Iranians. The controversy over the naming
of the Persian Gulf is one example; it consistently drew massive online
participation from the earliest days of the Iranian Internet and is perceived as an assault on the history and contemporary place of Iran.

   As part of its broader project of mobilizing the Internet in response
to the National Geographic Society's decision to offer two names for

the gulf in the eighth edition of its world atlas, the Ministry of Culture and Islamic Guidance launched the online Persian Gulf Festival,
which prominently featured a blogging competition.[28] Unlike the
"Imam Khomeini and Youth" competition, this one did not betray an
openly ideological stance other than to appeal to Iranian nationalism
in the most visceral sense. In this case, the state was not only able to
ride the wave of nationalistic fury against the publication but also to
co-opt expressions of nationalism that were critical of the current ruling system. Reactions to the Persian Gulf controversy that were critical
of the Iranian state were effectively defanged, swept away by the government's own forceful and multifaceted response.

    Thus, while the government did take action against bloggers in this
period, its tactics in dealing with the blogosphere as a potential site of
dissent and political actions were not monolithic. Its repressive role in
filtering sites and singling out reformist journalists-turned-bloggers
for persecution was just one prong of its approach. Projects such as
the Persian Gulf Festival indicate that the state also used some of the
classic tactics of liberal democracies in dealing with dissent.

    In addition to staking claim to territory on the blogosphere and
attempting to direct and co-opt discourses produced on Weblogistan,
state institutions also participated in creating discourse about it. The
Ministry of Culture and Islamic Guidance's commissioning of several
studies devoted to the blogosphere provide an example of the state's
role in knowledge production about Weblogistan. In 2007, the Bureau
of Media Studies and Planning, an office of the Ministry of Culture,
published four reports about blog content that had been generated
over the previous two years.[29] The reports identify but do not explicitly
define two genres of blogs: the "political" and the "social." They also
use several categories for assessing the Iranian blogosphere: reformist,
Principalist, critical, and neutral. While the former two labels are self-
explanatory, the latter are far from self-evident. In addition, the studies do not allow for an overlap of categories and do not acknowledge
that a blog can be both "critical" and reformist or Principalist. Despite
this and many other shortcomings, the reports reflect both the diversity and transnational nature of Weblogistan, even if grudgingly so. In
other words, although the government's framework for assessing the
blogosphere may be skewed to underplay the role of dissenting blogs

and to emphasize the activities of bloggers who were sympathetic to the ruling system and to the administration in office at the time, the overall picture captures a dynamic blogosphere.

For example, the bureau's 2007 report found that the largest percentage of blogs written during the spring and summer of 2006 was "Neutral" (nearly 50 percent), followed by "Reformist" (20 percent), "Critical" (around 19 percent), and "Principalist" (slightly over 10 percent). Like ensuing reports, the study most clearly betrayed its political biases in its findings on Principalist and reformist blogs. Although the report claimed that the Principalists showed the "least fear" about revealing their identities, it also asserted that the reformists did not seem to worry about having their identities exposed either; 90 percent of the latter wrote under their real names. This lack of concern was not attributable to location, as the study (incredibly) claimed that no such blogs were produced outside the country.

This finding contrasts with the finding of the last report in the series, which covers blogs from spring 2007 to spring 2008. According to the latter report, all Principalist blogs were written under the blogger's real name whereas reformists were more likely to write anonymously. Betraying a rare slip from the objective language it attempted to follow, the last report also claimed that the reformist sites were more likely "to hide" their hit counters from the public. This breach is all the more evident when compared to the neutral language the study used to observe that Principalist blogs made the least use of hit counters. Finally, this last study noted that all Principalist blogs were written inside the country, no change was discerned in the location of reformist blogs compared to previous years, and the vast majority of "critical" blogs were written outside Iran.

The report did not draw explicit conclusions from these findings, but the implication seems to be clear: Principalist blogs are transparent, written by real persons with real names who reside inside the country and who are therefore more authentic and accountable. While this is likely the conclusion the ministry may prefer, the report's finding can be interpreted in a way that is more sympathetic to the reformist and critical blogs: if the Principalist bloggers write openly from Iran, it may say more about their proximity to power than about any inherent tendency toward transparency.[30] In other words, the report's findings can be read as a confirmation, rather than a rebuttal, of some of the major tenets of mainstream discourses: that the blogosphere is a site for evading repressive government measures and that Iran offers full free speech rights to only the most ardent supporters of the ruling system. But whatever their flaws and intentions, the reports ultimately reflect a diverse Weblogistan with transnational and translocal points of origin and exchange.

At least one other aspect of these reports should be highlighted. In its findings on the 2006 blogosphere, the ministry noted a decline in Weblogistan, a trend that its 2008 study confirmed. Although the 2008 study qualified this by claiming that Weblogistan had "matured," its conclusions about an impending decline may explain why the ministry provided no further studies of the blogosphere on the Web site of the Bureau of Media Studies and Planning. Indeed, as subsequent chapters will show, the state adjusts its approach to changes online, allocating resources where it locates the greatest potential impact in the production of discourses on and about cyberspace.

Yet the state is also prone to miscalculate and overplay its hand. These moments are particularly instructive because they raise the ire of both oppositional figures and those who ostensibly share the principles of the administration and/or state agencies attempting to intervene in the blogosphere. As such, they also provide a lens for assessing the cracks and complexities of the political sphere. The Ministry of Culture's project called "Organizing Websites and Weblogs" is one such instance.

In 2006, the presidential cabinet approved a plan put forth by the deputy minister of culture that would have required all bloggers and Web site owners to register their sites with the ministry.[31] The text of the bylaws that were passed contains the justification for this extraordinary step in interfering in the blogosphere: "A—The People's right to free and healthy access to information and knowledge; B—Support for legal sites spreading information; C—Respect for social rights and the protection of the country's Islamic, national, cultural, and social views. D—The civil and criminal liability of persons for their activities."[32]

The rest of the regulations include the customary definition of terms, the duties of the ministry in relation to the new plan, and

restrictions on what might be expressed online and how violations
would be addressed. In short, the ministry cast itself as a champion of
free speech at the same time that it was attempting to curb it and justified the proposed limitations by appealing to a shared set of religious
and national values. Indeed, this dual language of claiming support
for a set of rights with the caveat that they could not cross certain
lines is characteristic of many laws and regulations in Iran. Thus, this
proposal can be seen as a rather clumsy attempt to overlay existing
mechanisms for monitoring and controlling information onto the
blogosphere and the Internet more broadly.

Less than six months after passing the bylaws, the Ministry of Culture and Islamic Guidance gave bloggers and Web site owners a two-
month window to register their sites, a move that attracted immediate
media attention inside and outside Iran.[33] Given its potential impact
on Weblogistan, the plan received a series of negative responses even
before the bylaws were passed. These reactions to the plan were not
surprising, especially among bloggers who were explicitly opposed to
the administration or to the ruling system in its entirety. Yet criticism
of the proposal was not limited to the usual quarters, and the ministry's ill-fated project is among the few issues that garnered a kind of
consensus in an otherwise highly fractured blogosphere. For example,
blogger Yek Hezbollahi, whose name (a follower of Iranian Hezbol-
lah) leaves no doubt about his political leanings, noted:

> When I first heard about the plan to organize blogs, I didn't take
> it very seriously. . . . After all, we and they have something called
> brains and thoughts! How could they decide to control *this* many
> blogs? . . . The principle of the plan is not problematic. Having a
> website shouldn't be as easy as it is and probably that is what [the
> ministry] meant. For some, blogs are like a diary. For some, blogs
> are for passing the time. How many daily readers do most blogs
> have that they should be controlled? Of what importance is our
> childishness? Registering blogs is ridiculous. That is why some are
> saying: "If you give your diary to more than three people, then send
> a copy to the Ministry of Culture and Islamic Guidance." . . . They
> should have never talked about blogs to begin with. They could
> have said "websites" and defined boundaries for what they meant.
> These people from the ministry and the parliament either don't

know what blogs are and underestimate the power of blogs (ahem, ahem) or they are overly brave and have (censored) in their brains. Everywhere they have called this the plan to register website and blogs even in the registration forms, and then they say that the registration for blogs is voluntary! What is wrong with these people?[34]

Attacking the plan both for its impracticality and inconsistencies, the writer also makes two seemingly contradictory claims about blogs. On the one hand, he asserts that most are not substantial in terms of content or audience size, but on the other hand, he recognizes their potential for defying the ruling system. Indeed, as considered further below, the simple refusal of bloggers to register was a deciding factor in the plan's defeat. Furthermore, Yek Hezbollahi is not reserved in his criticism of those who supported the plan. Instead of scapegoating a weak link in the system, he targets entire governmental bodies for their ignorance. This latter point is important not only for what it shows about bloggers' negative reception of the plan but also for what it indicates about the blogosphere more generally: that Weblogistan, like the transnational societies to which it is linked, is too nuanced to be simply captured in terms of two camps who oppose or support the ruling system. At times, the harshest attacks come from those who are ostensible supporters.

Yet Hezbollahi's post was not atypical. A range of bloggers ridiculed the plan, but a few provided responses that were more serious. Alireza Shirazi, a blogger and programmer who is the head of the well-known Iran-based blog-hosting service Blogfa and the Persian search engine Parseek, provided a rigorous yet measured post outlining the problems with the plan. Shirazi argued that the bylaws' definition of "sites spreading information" is so broad as to "apply to everything that exists on the web." Shirazi also outlined redundancies in the bylaws, such as their goal of fighting illegal activities online, an issue that he noted was already handled under the supervision of several government organs such as the judiciary, the Ministry of Information and Communications Technology, and the Committee to Identify Computer Crimes. Finally, Shirazi pointed out the many difficulties that stood in the way of implementing the plan, given that "more than 1.5 million blogs are registered with Persian blog providers" and tens of thousands of other sites were hosted abroad.[35]

Beyond the jurisdiction obstacles for an organization attempting to impose the registration rules, the issue of foreign-hosted domains proved a major embarrassment for the ministry. In May 2006, news sources in Iran revealed that the ministry's own Web site for receiving registrations was hosted in New Jersey, adding caustically that the government was insisting on gathering identifying information from Netizens only to hand them over to authorities in the United States.[36] Concerns about the security of information provided through the registration program were further aggravated when the ministry's Web site was hacked several months after the exposé about its American domain host.[37]

The ministry's problems were compounded by the overwhelming refusal of bloggers and Web site owners to register. Soon after the announcement of the plan, bloggers openly declared that they would defy the call to provide their information. Many decorated their blogs with the logo "I will not register."[38] Ten days after registration began, news sources inside the country, including *Kayhan*, the daily newspaper notorious for its alignment with the hardline elements of the ruling system, ran stories about the negligible numbers of registrants.[39] Nearly half a year after the government's two-month deadline for registering sites had passed, Hamid Ziayee-Parvar, a blogger who openly identifies himself as a researcher with the ministry, noted on his personal blog: "In the most optimistic interpretation possible, only 1.5% of Iranian websites and blogs were willing to register their information with the ministry's organization plan. For a governmental plan that had the backing and leverage of power behind it, this counts as a defeat and the architects of this plan must be held accountable before the people in a press conference."[40]

The ministry's ill-conceived plan may have been doomed to failure from the outset, but its attempts to implement it and the widespread criticism it received are important for an understanding of the evolution of the Iranian Internet and Weblogistan in particular. The plan was the Iranian state's most ambitious effort to intervene online. Using the rhetoric of rights and values alongside bureaucratic justifications for "organization," the ministry crafted an unwieldy plan for controlling an even more unwieldy cyberspace. In short, the plan reveals the increasing importance the government accorded to Weblogistan and indicates a new phase in the development of its responses. In addition, the widespread opposition to the plan is significant not only because it effectively killed the project but also because critics used the medium of blogging as a site for resisting the plan and pointing out its flaws.

CONCLUSION

Weblogistan reached its peak within a few years of its establishment. It was home to contradictory sentiments, agendas, and political sensibilities, much like the complex offline spaces to which it was linked. The opportunities it offered for relatively sustained forms of transnational connectivity and for defying social and political taboos excited international observers as much as it alarmed the conflict-ridden Iranian state, which reacted by filtering blogs and (in some cases) persecuting individual bloggers. Yet this constituted but one component of the state's response as it quickly recognized the importance of shaping discourses on and about the blogosphere. Official organs of the state produced reports on the blogosphere, promoted the production of blog posts that buttressed its favored national narratives and experimented with new modes of managing the blogosphere. In short, the state moved along a spectrum of approaches to blogs, sometimes taking contradictory actions or proposing projects (such as the failed plan to force registration of blogs) that led to objections even from those who support the government.

For individual participants in Weblogistan, the field was similarly complex. The bloggers who are largely excluded from dominant accounts about the phenomenon belie the erroneous assumption that Weblogistan was a unified entity. This framework misses an opportunity to capture some of the bluntest critical assessments of the Iranian state and society in the Iranian online world. Weblogistan was large enough to accommodate a range of individual and official presences, the state's repressive measures notwithstanding.

As a medium, blogging made possible the convergence of various modes of textual and image-based expression as Internet technologies grew. One category of the image-based expressions—digitally distributed film and videos—merits consideration that goes beyond its uses in the blogosphere. As the Iranian Internet expanded, so too did the state's multifaceted involvement, and moving images provided many opportunities for it to manufacture and/or entrench official national narratives. But the same Internet technologies that strengthened the state's positions may also be used to undermine them. The next chapter explores these developments on the Iranian Internet.

CHAPTER 3

THE MOVABLE
IMAGE

Like the Iranian Internet, Iranian visual culture has received significant scholarly and mainstream attention. Discussions of Iranian visual
productions generally take care to situate their topic in the context of
postrevolutionary politics, often pointing out the challenges of cultural work and the opportunities it provides to traverse geographical
and social boundaries. Given the richness of this field, it is surprising
that more attention has not been paid to the intersection of moving
image cultures and the Iranian Internet.

Similarly, in studies of contemporary Iran more broadly, while the
Iran-Iraq war is generally recognized as significant for the mechanisms the Iranian state used to define itself, the centrality of cultural
productions has been largely overlooked in favor of accounts of the
power politics resulting from the war. While some recent scholarship
has turned its attention to visual cultures related to the Iran-Iraq war,
the focus has been on material that is made and distributed offline.
However, beginning in the early years of the new millennium, virtual
spheres rapidly caught up with offline cultural productions about the
war that were over twenty years in the making, most often in the form
of reproducing what had previously been available only in nondig-
ital forms. The reappearance of this material online does not mean
that the Iranian Internet acted as a mirror, merely providing a copy in
another format. Indeed, the reproduction and dissemination of digitized visual media on the Iranian Internet has presented new opportunities to both strengthen and challenge dominant narratives of the
Iran-Iraq war and its legacies in contemporary Iran.

The relative dearth of scholarship on digital films and videos may be explained by the timing of technological developments. By the time the ability to capture and disseminate moving images had become available to average users, the Iranian Internet had already exploded. YouTube, which appeared on the scene in 2005, offered individual users the opportunity to embed videos and made it possible for users to integrate digital films and videos on their Web sites and blogs. The easy assimilation of moving images into existing sites meant that films and videos could be included in discussions on blogs and other Web sites. However, in Iran, blogs and other text-heavy online platforms remained the favored platform for analysis during the first decade of the new millennium.

As has been the case with other aspects of the Iranian Internet, accounts of the use of digital visual technologies online have largely focused on how digital moving images have been used to challenge the state, for example what occurred in the wake of the disputed 2009 presidential election (Sabety 2010). The coincidence of the rise of social media with government crackdowns following the 2009 election inspired many popular reflections on how digital videos were used to gain transnational support for demonstrators and to document violence against protesters. Many of these celebratory accounts hailed the "citizen journalist" and his or her savvy in capturing and distributing digital moving images.[1] However, some analysts have looked a bit deeper at this new use of technology and are concerned about the ethics of this new terrain. Mette Mortensen, for example, has studied how journalists used the footage of the death of Neda Agha Soltan, who was killed during the protests in 2009, to consider the ethics of the uses of this material (Mortensen 2011). From an entirely different but nonetheless critical perspective, Setrag Manoukian has applied Giorgio Agamben's notion of "the contemporary" to how the demonstrators referenced Iran's revolutionary past and to YouTube videos of the protests (Manoukian 2010).

Similarly, most accounts of state action in this period focus on its use of repressive mechanisms, which is not surprising, since state forces are at their most aggressive during moments of heightened crisis. The analysis of the use of digital film and video during times of unrest, most of which has come from journalists, is important for understanding local and transnational uses of digital media in relation to political developments in Iran. But a fuller grasp of the role of moving images on the Iranian Internet requires an examination of how they are used in broader contexts.

New capacities for producing and circulating digital moving images—especially via popular platforms with an international reach—have had mixed consequences. They have vastly expanded the state's efforts to push particular narratives about the war and its legacy. At the same time, new platforms for distribution make these narratives vulnerable to challenges that reach broad audiences. Similarly, individuals may repurpose war-related materials in ways that deviate from official uses and in many cases explicitly subvert them. The ability to make and share audiovisual materials online opened new fields for both constructing and contesting core aspects of Iranian society and national identity, including the identity and role of the Diaspora. These processes are particularly important in relation to material pertaining to the Iran-Iraq war, given the continued resonance of the conflict.

This chapter begins with an overview of state-endorsed material about the Iran-Iraq war, focusing on items produced and/or recirculated from 2004 to 2010. In the first years of this period, the state and its institutions had an advantage over individual users because of the high level of skill and resources posting audiovisual materials online required. This changed with the advent of free and global platforms for distributing such content.

War Productions Offline: Constructing the Memory and Legacy of the "Sacred Defense"

There is a general consensus in the scholarship on postrevolutionary Iran that the Iran-Iraq war played an important role in enabling the newly formed government to define itself and consolidate its power. Iran was still at the height of its postrevolutionary turmoil when Iraq invaded, and the war presented a timely crisis for the newly forming Islamic Republic. It provided a reason for calls for unity and made it easier for the government to eliminate scores of rivals in the new power structure. But the war also benefited the state's project of self-establishment and self-definition in ways that went beyond its immediate and pragmatic goal of meeting challenges from within. The new state recognized the power of images and symbols and supported the production and dissemination of various forms of cultural products, from songs composed to support the war effort to films that chronicled it. The voices of devotional singer Sadeq Ahangaran and Gholamali Koveitipoor became familiar through repeated exposure on state television and radio. State television also ran the 63-episode documentary series *Ravayat Ne Fath* [The story of victory], directed by Morteza Aviny. The war was officially referred to as the "Imposed War" and/or the "Sacred Defense,"[2] and murals, Friday prayer sermons, newspapers and other publications, radio programs, and audiovisual productions did the work of framing and entrenching the official narrative of the conflict as it unfolded.

War-related propaganda did not end with the conflict's termination in 1988. State-sponsored signifiers of the period—streets named after martyrs, commemorative murals, films, and television series—seek to preserve the war as a living memory, even for the segment of the population that is too young to have lived through it. Indeed, a steady stream of material became available after the war ended and continued through the early years of the new millennium, when the number of such products spiked. Morteza Aviny continued to work on war documentaries until he died in 1993 while on a production site with his crew. His death occurred on a former battlefield when he accidentally stepped on a mine, earning him the status of "martyr" and cementing his place as the revered documentarian of the war. Numerous lesser-known documentaries have been made with official blessings in Iran, some of which have aired on state channels. The Documentary Channel (established in 2009) has taken a lead role in broadcasting and supporting this material. Indeed, in 2012, the deputy director of the state broadcasting announced that the head of the Documentary Channel had been tasked with making the "biggest, most thorough, and [most] comprehensive" film about the war.[3]

In addition to documentary works, films that deal with the war and its legacy have been a consistent part of the Iranian cinema industry. According to Richard Tapper (2002), over fifty films were made during the conflict, and the war continued to be a popular subject in the 1990s and into the new millennium. That these films have not been restricted to dramas is somewhat surprising, since the material and psychological effects of the war continue to be felt twenty years after its end. Several comedies centered on the war, most notably Masoud Dehnamaki's popular film *Ekhrajiha* [The Outcasts], which has spawned two sequels at the time of this writing. Although both fiction and documentary works relating to the Sacred Defense have been largely overshadowed in English-language accounts by international festival circuit films of celebrated directors, they have increasingly come to the attention of scholars since the new millennium (Abecassis 2011; Khosronejad 2012; Varzi 2002; Varzi 2006; Vatanabadi 2009).

The abundance of audiovisual material about the war is matched by a range of publications. A flood of fiction and nonfiction accounts of the war as experienced by soldiers and their female relatives has been well received by the reading public.[4] Poetry collections memorializing the war continued to be published in the postwar period.[5] A smaller subset of books about the conflict chronicle and analyze it from historical and political perspectives (Doroodian 1993; Doroodian 1994; Kamari 2008; Sameei 1993). The number of publications on the topic is so large that a multivolume compilation of annotated bibliographies has been published (Boroumand 2005). A similar work that catalogs films and videos related to the Iran-Iraq war is also available, published by the Islamic Republic Broadcasting Services (Paravar 1994). In addition, the promotion and dissemination of Sacred Defense music continues, in no small part due to official support in various forms, including the Provincial Sacred Defense Music Festival, which began in 2004. The government has also sponsored poetry festivals and theater festivals on the theme.

Improvements in Internet technology in Iran made it possible for individuals to supplement the explosion in cultural products about the Iran-Iraq war with online content that promoted offline materials and, to a lesser extent, created new content. Although much of the virtual material on the war is produced by individual or independent sources, the vast majority is explicitly or indirectly supported by the government. Thus, this online content is further evidence of the state's expanding use of the Internet as an arena for exercising nonrepressive forms of power. At the same time, online digitized material, particularly audiovisual content, is open to broader communities of interpretation and can be repurposed in ways that challenge the ruling powers' prevailing narratives.

DIGITIZED WAR: RECONSTRUCTING A CONFLICT ONLINE

The noticeable appearance of war-related material online roughly coincided with the state's increasing recognition of the ways the Internet could be used proactively. The Martyr Aviny Institute of Culture and Art, whose funding comes from a combination of state and private sources,[6] was among the first to establish itself as an online source for material related to the war. As early as 2003, the Aviny.com site housed a range of resources, including audio and visual content. While the site was formed to draw attention to the productions and person of celebrated war documentarian Morteza Aviny, it has from its earliest days provided other content, including material broadly related to the war and the country's revolutionary past, religious materials, and current news. This triad, familiar from offline depictions of the war, reappears in most of the materials it provides online. Scholars have often commented on the centrality of religious narratives, particularly the story of Karbala, to the government's official accounts of the war as it unfolded and to its memorialization once it had ended (Khosronejad, 2013; Moallem 2005; Varzi 2006). While tropes related to Karbala continue to appear in war-related materials, the religion node of the triad has diversified over the years to include a broader range of content, from Quranic verses to the speeches and lives of members of the clergy. Similarly, analysis and news of current events has expanded to reflect the interests and agendas of individuals or organizations covering war-related content online. In the case of the Aviny Institute's Web site, this includes local and international news, articles on society and culture, and political analyses that indicate the institute's alignment with hardline elements of the ruling system. The tendency to link memorializations of the war to contemporary figures is evidence of the continuing importance of the conflict to the ruling powers' processes of self-definition and assertions of political legitimacy.

The Aviny Institute is far from the only organization to have taken its work on the war online. A number of government and government-supported entities created to promote the "culture of sacrifice and

Figure 8. A 2003 screen capture of the introduction page of the Aviny Institute's Web site, one of the most well developed in Iran at the time. The site included audio and flash animation.

martyrdom" have established Web sites to memorialize the war. The Secretariat for the Coordination and Oversight of the Promotion of the Culture of Sacrifice and Martyrdom has been online since 2003. In June of that year, the site put out a call for contributions from readers, promising "valuable prizes" for the best articles. Throughout 2003, the secretariat elicited reader participation, including putting out a call that year and in subsequent years for readers who were willing to serve as official reporters.[7] According to the title of the bylaws that established the secretariat, its mission also includes "upholding the memory of martyrs and celebrating those who sacrificed for the Sacred Defense and providing cultural-artistic facilities for the honored families of martyrs and those who have sacrificed."[8] Given this mandate, the site primarily functions to highlight news about activities that honor or support war veterans and martyrs. Similar to the Aviny Institute but on a smaller scale, the secretariat's Web site includes war-related images that can be easily downloaded and recirculated.

Both sites also promote new publications related to the war, but neither makes them available for free or as paid downloads, thus limiting their function to promotion. The government may support such content and producers may generate it for ideological reasons, but like other cultural goods, a significant proportion of material about the war is available only to paying customers. The popularity of war-themed books and films and online content about the war demonstrates the public's appetite for the topic as a form of leisure activity, underscoring the idea that such products cannot be merely dismissed as propaganda, even if they have also served this purpose.

The Aviny Institute and the secretariat are just two examples of state or state-supported organizations dedicated to the war and its veterans, but they stand out because of the emphasis they place on culture and cultural production.[9] Their appearance online indicates that they recognize the importance of expanding the boundaries of the cultural endeavor to memorialize and mobilize the war, and they must be read as part of the state's broader plans for establishing its presence on the Iranian Internet.

The case of the Rasekhoon Web site, which is produced by the Noor Rasekhoon Art and Cultural Institute, is very instructive in this regard. Its extensive "About Us" section is remarkable for several reasons.[10] First, it is transparent in stating that it is funded by the government-sponsored Sazeman-e Oqaf va Omoor-e Kheirey-e (The Religious Endowment and Charity Organization) and indicates that in 2008, the Web site had received the blessing of the Supreme Leader Ayatollah Khamenei. Perhaps most importantly, the Web site explicitly frames its goals in terms of producing culture: "One of the most valuable goals of the Islamic Republic is the production and expansion of knowledge and culture-building in the correct Islamic manner. In this regard, media have an effective and constructive role and each work as an instrument to produce and transfer culture among various groups in society. Among these, as the newest and most modern mass communication instruments, Web sites and portals play the most important role."[11]

In outlining how it fulfills this role, the organization's lengthy "About Us" section is divided under headings such as research in religion and other religious themes. It also includes the Iran-Iraq war under the heading of culture. A similar categorization of Sacred Defense material can be found on the Tebyan Web site.[12] Also openly sponsored by the government, this site—which has been around since 2002—shares with Rasekhoon an emphasis on the importance of producing culture. It too includes extensive material on the Sacred Defense, offering audiovisual content on the topic for streaming.

Figure 9. The Web site Rasekhoon offers audio and audiovisual content on the topic of "Sacred Defense" for streaming and download. The site also contains prominent ads that link to political documentaries about Iran's former king and the Mujahedin-e Khalq organization.

In addition, hundreds of blogs are solely devoted to the war. Many of these began in 2004. It is likely no accident that this is the year that the number of published memoirs and fictional accounts related to the eight-year conflict spiked. While these blogs are ostensibly independent, they must be read both in relation to the explosion of offline content and state-supported production of material online.[13] Discussions of the war and its legacy are also evident on blogs that are not expressly devoted to the issue. These have been largely produced by those who self-identify as religious and who often express allegiance to the ruling system. However, this positionality does not always translate into an affinity with government-favored narratives; these bloggers have offered some of the most biting critiques of the conflict's legacy, especially the current situation of veterans (Akhavan 2011). Whatever their particular take on the conflict, the countless blogs that are devoted to the war open new forums for virtual content production and circulation, including audiovisual content.[14]

The cultural products about the Iran-Iraq war have also included small but solid forays into the field of critical publications that were available both in hard copy and online. Ventures with little or no institutional support have also established themselves online. The

self-described nongovernmental and nonpartisan student journal
Habil, which began a limited publication run in 2006, provided free
access to html and pdf versions of its journal on its Web site along with
resources such as bibliographies about material on the Iran-Iraq War.[15]
According to its "About Us" section, the publication understands itself
as unique among publications about the war because it is produced
by those without firsthand experiences of the conflict. If *Habil'*s work
is any indication, the new generation of writers about the war is both
more critical and more creative than the generation that preceded it
and has benefited from temporal and geographical distance from the
war. The appearance of such materials online expanded the interpre-
tive community, offering challenges to the state's monopoly on narratives of the war.

In its inaugural issue, entitled "The People's Sacred Defense, the
Government's Sacred Defense," the journal made a useful distinction
between the two discourses indicated in its title. The latter discourse
consists of narratives that are "favorable to the rulers and politicians
and [are] based on their policies," while the former discourse is narrated by the people, "meaning the real players in the imposed war. . . .
Put another way, the people's Sacred Defense is the real and eyewitness
account of the war as it was while the government's Sacred Defense is
the narrative of the war that should have been" (Mazahery 2006, 4). The
fact that the government often supports the production of narratives by
"the people" blurs the line between the two, but nonetheless Mazahery's
distinction can be usefully applied to assessments of the intersection of
cultural production about the war and Internet technologies. Some of
*Habil'*s efforts and many of the blogs covering the war can be seen as
highlighting "the people's" Sacred Defense alongside their engagement
with official discourses. The Iranian Internet, especially its spaces that
circulate audiovisual materials, provides opportunities for new interro-
gations of the multiple narratives of the war.[16]

GLOBAL PLATFORM, LOCAL WAR: CIRCULATION OF
OFFICIAL MATERIALS IN UNOFFICIAL SPACES

The nature of "people's" online productions about the war, like all
other content on the Iranian Internet, must be read in relation to

interlinked social and technological developments. Some forms of creative expression about the war, such as memoirs, stories, and poetry, do not require extraordinary Internet capacities and can be easily produced and/or disseminated on Web sites and blogs. Many of the war blogs mentioned above, for example, began during the rising tide of Web 2.0 technologies. In that period, sharing audiovisual content required more skill and resources, which likely explains why only well-funded and experienced organizations such as the Aviny Institute could include it on their Web sites. The appearance of video-sharing Web sites in 2005 opened opportunities for individual users to participate in the production and dissemination of audiovisual content.[17]

On free and popular platforms such as YouTube, users can participate creatively, even in when they merely reproduce existing content. The ability to provide descriptions and tag materials and embed videos in blogs and on other Web sites provides numerous opportunities for users to actively frame content. In addition, while blogs and other Web sites carrying war-related content—especially those, such as the Aviny site, that occasionally offer materials in multiple languages—are theoretically capable of engaging transnational audiences, internationally popular platforms such as YouTube increase the likelihood that shared content will reach a broader viewership. This is attributable to the combination of YouTube's global popularity, the algorithms it uses to provide suggestions to viewers watching any particular video, and its various social networking features, all of which have made YouTube attractive to users around the world.[18]

YouTube's global reach and the options it offers participants opened the floodgates for media that addressed the war. The rise of video sharing was both productive and disruptive for individuals and organizations with an interest in various uses of the Iran-Iraq war, and the practice adds complexity to the rich field of cultural productions relating to the conflict.

Although YouTube is not the only site that allows Iranian Internet users access to audiovisual material related to the Iran-Iraq war, its specific characteristics create unique consequences for discourses relating to the conflict. Films and videos about the war on Iranian Web sites tend to appear in limited or controlled environments. Pages affiliated with officially sanctioned Web sites in Iran reflect the latter tendency: although they have an advantage over sites such as YouTube because they enable users to easily download material, they provide little or no opportunity for direct audience engagement. In addition, because these texts appear within the boundaries of the preselected context designed by the administrators, the possibilities for multiple interpretations of the materials presented are limited. In contrast, platforms such as YouTube offer magnified opportunities for both entrenching and undermining narratives of the war that have been privileged in Iran since its outbreak in 1980. A closer look at several examples illustrates how this has been the case.

Two of the most frequently viewed uploads that YouTube retrieves with the Persian search terms *Defa-e moqadas* (Sacred Defense), were made by a user named Aminamiens, whose profile notes a location in France.[19] These two videos were uploaded under titles in both English and Persian and have been viewed over 200,000 times. Neither clip is original; both are government-produced pieces. One is about the war effort in general and the other was made for the anniversary of the liberation of Khorramshahr from Iraqi forces. Both are set to the music of devotional and war anthem singer Sadeq Ahangaran.[20] The user has imprinted his own name and Web site address on both, but that is the extent of his mark on the clips. That is to say, he has made no effort to alter the clips or to frame them with descriptions and tags. Thus, he has merely reproduced state-sponsored material without detracting from the original message of the clips in any way. This cannot be said of the hundreds who have responded to the videos. The majority of Iranians writing in Persian and English expressed appreciation for the sacrifices of soldiers, but some users crossed the thin line between nationalistic pride and racism, provoking similarly hateful responses from some Iraqi or other Arab users.

While such outbursts are rare, they disrupt the carefully crafted official narrative of the war, which located the enemy in the person of Saddam and the Ba'ath Party and avoided constructions that played on Sunni-Shia, Arab-Persian, or other dichotomies. Similarly, the state's heavy-handed use of tropes from Shi'ism—such as its support for the popular song "Karbala, ma dareem miyaeem" (Karbala we are coming), which accompanies Aminamiens's most frequently viewed video—stayed clear of antagonizing Sunnis. Although Iran is

Figure 10. One of the most frequently viewed clips retrieved on YouTube
using the Persian search terms for "Sacred Defense." The audiovisual content
was produced with Iranian state support during the Iran-Iraq war and has
not been altered by the uploader.

a Shia-majority nation with a government rooted in Ayatollah Khomeini's interpretation of a form of state that is in harmony with Shia
tenets, it also contains a sizable Sunni minority, including most of the
three million Arabs in the country, most of whom live in the war-torn
areas. Any explicit references to sect or ethnicity would risk alienating
significant portions of the population and would contradict Ayatollah
Khomeini's shift from his early sectarian views to a view that favored
Muslim unity. In any case, the state depended on the war to promote
a national narrative that bolstered its place as a defender of a vulnerable nation. Drawing attention to national difference—sectarian,
linguistic, or otherwise—would have undermined this project. In the
open field of YouTube, individual viewers easily breach these boundaries, steering the conversation toward controversial topics that state-
supported discourse on the war assiduously avoids. On the YouTube
page where Aminamiens's popular video accompanied by Ahangaran's voice appeared, for example, commenters heatedly debated the
merits of Sunnism or Shi'ism. One user named Sirwallaby used the
song's appeal to Karbala as evidence of Shi'a apostasy: "So sad instead
of calling for god they call for a city in iraq and hussian RA. . . . no
wonder shia are not considered muslims anymore."[21]

In these comments, the entire war was subject to debate. The per-
sonalities and leadership of Khomeini and Saddam, the responsibility for starting and maintaining the war, and the complicity of other
nations in assisting Iraq with its invasions were all intensely interro-
gated. Even Iranians who praised the country's ability to endure dis-
agreed with each other about the role of Islam in motivating soldiers
on the front lines. For example, Andishmandan, who was angry with a
fellow commenter who had apparently questioned the importance of
religion, posted a response that made his vexation clear through abbre-
viations and an unorthodox use of capitalization: "these people are in
love of there iran and islam. They fought and gave all they had, there
belief, life and land was all they had and they used it to free IRAN!
Not like your parents who ran away to America and called themselves
Michael and David and became 'I am Persian'! And we dont need
ppl like you to come and give shit comments. Again the hosseins and
mohammads of iran from the downtown and small cities and ppl you
call 'dahati' [peasants] will defend IRAn if it is ever in danger. NOT u!!"
    Exchanges such as this get at the core of what is at stake in con-
temporary discourse about the Iran-Iraq war: the identity and political leanings of those who were on the front lines. In Iran, some have
claimed connections to martyrs or veterans as a means of identifying
themselves with the heroism of those who defended the country, a
strategy that state-sponsored cultural products seem to have been following since the outset of the war. Put another way, claiming participation in or a familial link to the war equates to having legitimacy as a
true heir of the nation. The state's use of and assertions of support for
martyrs and their families are some of the mechanisms it uses to cap-
italize on national goodwill toward the memory of those who fought
in the war.
    It is important to note that Andishmandan's comment does more
than indicate divisions of opinion about the identity and motivations
of soldiers; it also exposes fissures in the national fabric that extend to
the Diaspora. While digital technologies have provided nonresident
Iranians with opportunities to engage with issues pertaining to their
homeland, the importance of physical presence in particular locations
remains relevant. In Andishmandan's comment, leaving the country, changing one's name, and calling oneself "Persian" rather than

"Iranian" are taken as indications that the émigré has rejected Iran while largely poor and religious individuals have stayed behind to fight. If participating in the eight-year war is the epitome of courage and resilience in defense of the country, then anyone who would not or could not participate may be easily cast as cowardly and unfaithful. In the arena of state politics, this logic is used as a mechanism for enhancing one's power and demeaning one's rivals.

Paradoxically, however, the war also acts as national glue, providing a sense of shared pride in the country's ability to hold its own during the conflict. This dynamic is apparent on the transnational stage and is most easily observed in the multimedia spaces created by YouTube and the like. At the same time, physical location remains an issue in determinations of loyalty. Another example of this can be seen under the video entitled "14 Year old Soldier," posted in 2006, which has been viewed more than 200,000 times.[22] The clip, an interview with a fourteen-year-old boy and his companions who joined the war effort, originally aired on state television and then reappeared on the video-sharing site Iran Negah, which the uploader has credited as the source in the title.[23] A subtitle in the original clip indicates that the main interviewee, Mehrdad Azizollahi, was killed in the war.

Like the two videos posted by Aminamiens, the clip of Azizollahi engendered heated exchanges about the war. Many of the nearly 2,000 commenters focused on the meaning and morality of using child soldiers. As with all videos about the war, users writing in both Persian and English praised the sacrifices of those participating in the war. At least one commenter, posting under the username Jasonthemankiller, framed this admiration in relation to Diasporic Iranians: "wow i love this kid what a MAN wouldn't trade hem for miljons of those Iranian traitors who fled Iran when we was under attack." Once again, participation in the war and physical presence in the country is seen as the mark of a true patriot.

Expressions of praise for national resilience that come at the expense of the Diaspora trouble visions of the Internet as a space for strengthening a sense of Iranian pride that transcends geographical borders. Yet such disruptive moments must be considered alongside the ways that the digital distribution of audiovisual materials about the war create powerful opportunities for transnational and transgenerational

gatherings around a defining national event. In creating what Miyase
Christensen and Christian Christensen have called "ephemeral communicative spaces" (Christensen and Christensen 2008; Christensen
2009), YouTube allows individuals who may not have been exposed
to the conflict because of age or location to take an active role in its
memorialization.

Iranian participants are not the only ones who discuss the war or
challenge dominant narratives about it. Although Iraqis and other
Arabs or Muslims occasionally participate by commenting on videos
posted in support of Iranian efforts, they are generally far outnumbered by American participants. This is particularly the case for video
uploads that include descriptive information in English. Uploads
with identifying material exclusively in Persian tend to draw fewer
comments from members of the Diaspora and/or non-Iranians. In
the broader international context, which includes over thirty years
of tensions between Iran and the United States and numerous ongoing U.S. wars in the Middle East, it is not surprising that responses
from Americans often diverge into debates about the past and present
involvement of the United States in the region. In some cases, the conversations become almost exclusively U.S.-centric in ways that seem to
make the Iran-Iraq war almost irrelevant. For example, the video entitled "Iraqi Republican Guard T-72 hunted down,"[24] which has been
viewed more than 600,000 times since it was posted in February 2007,
is a clip of footage originally broadcast by Iranian state television.
Although some commenters express admiration for or belittle the soldiers, very few of the over 1,500 comments appear to be from Iranians
or directly refer to that war. Instead, much muscle flexing takes place
between those who claim to support or have participated in the U.S.
wars with Iraq and those who oppose U.S. involvement.

From the perspective of the Iranian state's project of narrativiz-
ing and memorializing the war, the consequences of global platforms
such as YouTube are mixed. On the one hand, prior to the appearance
of such video-sharing sites, material produced by the Iranian state
could not be disseminated as far and as widely as it now is by individual users from around the world, most of whom appear to have
no affiliation—and likely even oppose—the current Iranian government. Vast distribution, however, comes at a price: materials become

subject to the open interrogation of a broad range of interpreters, with unpredictable consequences for accounts that are officially promoted by the Iranian state. While criticisms of U.S. military in the comments associated with some videos related to the Iran-Iraq war may fit with the state's position, the questioning and even the ridicule of Iran's performance during that war certainly do not.

Iran's state organs have the means to influence both production and the contexts of reception in the nation's media landscape. The recirculation of war-related materials crosses the boundaries the state has constructed around them, making it accessible to audiences whose responses may undermine as well as reinforce official narratives. Comments sections are not the only place where such responses take place. YouTube's algorithm for suggesting videos and its practice of highlighting promoted or featured material on the side of the screen introduce viewers to a range of videos they might not otherwise select. The videos that YouTube's sidebar promotes might not share the political orientation of the video the user is watching or even be in any way relevant to it. As the videos promoted in the sidebar are constantly changing, those who upload videos cannot attempt to preemptively address material that appears on the sidebar. In other words, users who upload videos have no way of predicting what will appear as suggestions to their viewers: a user uploading pro-state videos cannot include a note in her own upload about the specifics of what her viewers might see in the sidebars. Similarly, a user viewing a "favorited" video with a stable URL can expect to find a new permutation of sidebar materials with each visit.

Thus, the contexts of interpretation are in a constant state of flux. During one visit to the video entitled "Defa-e moqadas: Karbala ma dareem miyaeem [Sacred Defense: Karbala we are coming],"[25] for example, a video entitled "The Iran-Iraq War" in English and simply "The Iran War" in Arabic was the featured item in the side column.[26] The clip, which has been viewed well over 100,000 times, is made up entirely of stock footage from the war, and the source seems to be Iraqi television broadcasts. The video contains no diagetic sound and is oddly set to classical music, but at the very beginning, notes in English on the screen have been added to the edited stock footage as a sort of introduction. The clip begins with Saddam Hussein speaking, but most of the scenes are of Iraqi soldiers actively engaged in battle and making their way into Iran, including one scene of a soldier spray-painting "The Baath is our path" on Iranian road signs. The video, in short, provides a window on the war as it was broadcast on the other side of the border. Thus, a viewer who begins her YouTube experience with a clip celebrating the resilience of Iranian soldiers is only one click away from another video that shows the bravery of the soldiers on the other side. Of course, like the videos showing an Iranian perspective, this piece is also subject to challenge and reaffirmation through the comments section and the video clips that appear in its sidebar. YouTube provides the mechanism for such opposing visions to collide in ways that are unlikely to occur in any other virtual or offline space.

ALTERED STATES: WAR PRODUCTIONS REMIXED

State-endorsed materials about the war included an aural component. Whether in the form of performed poetry by Mohammad Reza Aghassi or the war songs of Sadeq Ahangaran and Gholamali Koveitipoor, war audio appeared alone or alongside visuals on Iran's state-owned broadcasting during the war and thereafter. This material has since become widely available in streaming or downloadable form on various Web sites, blogs, and video-sharing sites. Not surprisingly, songs routinely appear as the soundtrack to online videos commemorating the war. Although at first sight the recirculation of such materials in a global setting seems like a straightforward expansion of the state's narrative, the appearance of these materials in transnational settings may have complex consequences. Videos that weave original war-related audio or audiovisual materials into content that has few or no links to the eight-year conflict or its memorialization further complicate the picture. This phenomenon can be broadly separated into two categories: the first is comprised of videos that have few or no apparent connections to Iran, much less the Iran-Iraq war; the second consists of videos that arise out of an Iranian context and self-consciously remix war materials as part of a political agenda.

Several users posting in Turkish have used Koveitipoor's war anthem "Chang-e Del" in contexts that are unrelated to the Iran-Iraq war. A video approximately six-and-a-half minutes long that was posted in 2008, for example, begins with an edited sequence of stills and posters that show Chechen fighters praying, planning operations, or dead in battle alongside images of dead children, crying women, and displaced families.[27] About halfway through, the piece unexpectedly transitions to similar scenes of mayhem and sorrow associated with Palestine and Hamas, with occasional stills from Iraq and Chechnya as the song winds down. No reference to Iran, the revolution, or Iranian state ideology appears anywhere in the visuals, in the written text of the upload, or in the comments. While using the song to accompany a video focused exclusively on Palestine (as considered in the next case) may have some affinity with the Iranian state, given its rhetorical investment in the issue of Palestine, even this tenuous connection cannot be made in the case of Chechnya. Although the Iranian government has often spoken in defense of Islam-inspired movements, its relationship with Russia and its fear of separatist movements may explain its silence about Chechnya. While it is unlikely that the presumably Turkish-speaking intended audience of the video understands the song or its significance to the Iran-Iraq war, its juxtaposition with scenes of resistance captures the spirit of the work in a way that is similar to how it was originally intended. The song has been used in Iran as a motivating anthem for a war effort that was narrativized in terms of a David-versus-Goliath effort, and it functions the same way in relation to the depictions of Chechens and Palestinians.

The reappearance of state-endorsed cultural products about the war in unrelated contexts does not subvert the Iranian state's narratives about the conflict or about itself. An informed viewer may read the application of "Chang-e Del" to the Chechen situation as ironic, given that the state's rhetoric of solidarity with Muslim struggles has largely failed to mention what has been taking place north of its borders. However, this is clearly not the spirit behind the clip, and those who offered comments on the YouTube page that hosted it did not demonstrate an awareness of the context necessary to discern these potentially jarring moments. Although such videos may offer no significant challenge to official Iranian accounts of the war, they do not have a reaffirming function either.

Figure 11. A YouTube video about Palestinian militant groups that uses one of the Persian-language songs affiliated with the Sacred Defense in Iran. The accompanying text is in Turkish and the video was posted by a Turkish user.

A similar dynamic is at work in another item uploaded by a Turkish user who used the same song to accompany images related to Palestine, with a specific focus on Hamas. This clip has a fleeting visual reference to Iran—an image of Ayatollah Khomeini flashes on the screen at the outset—but the remainder focuses on Palestine and all the descriptive texts appear in Turkish.[28] Again, a thematic harmony exists between the song and the images displayed, but this time without irony, since the Iranian state has been open in its support for Hamas. Yet this compatibility and the image of Ayatollah Khomeini flitting across the screen do not constitute meaningful engagement with Iranian state ideologies and thus cannot be read as either clearly disrupting or reinforcing its narratives about the Iran-Iraq war.

No such ambiguity exists with videos that remix content linked to the war but directly engage issues related to Iran and have a clear aim to challenge the state. The best examples of such videos were uploaded in relation to the disputed presidential election of 2009 and the amorphous Green Movement that took shape in its wake. Several of the best-known anthems of the Iran-Iraq war, including "Chang-e Del," have accompanied images associated with the activities of the Green Movement and the various forms of state violence to which its members have been subject.[29] One of the most popular war anthems that

Figure 12. This video's soundtrack uses a Sacred Defense song that is most often affiliated with commemorations of fallen soldiers during the Iran-Iraq War. The YouTube user has repurposed it to commemorate the lives lost in the aftermath of the disputed 2009 election.

reappeared in relation to the post-2009 opposition is Koveitipoor's "Gharibane," a song lamenting the loss of comrades. It was originally composed in remembrance of the Iran-Iraq war dead, and it has had an online life in this capacity; popular video clips mix the song with various scenes from the war.[30] Yet the song has also resurfaced in relation to those who were killed in the aftermath of the 2009 election, and several videos used the song as a tribute to the fallen.[31]

Such uses of war-related cultural materials constitutes a direct challenge to the state in several ways. The language and imagery of martyrdom have been used in these videos, effectively wresting from the state its ability to define who constitutes a martyr. The establishment's carefully promoted account of the war and its legacy has relied on an aggressor/victim binary that placed the state on the side of those besieged by an oppressive invading force. In these clips, it is the state forces that are responsible for inflicting violence on the thousands of people who appear at demonstrations. And if the use of war songs with scenes of protest and the names of protesters who were under attack were not a clear enough rebuttal to the state's grip on the war narrative, the comments section that accompany these videos often make these connections explicit. In a number of cases, commenters assert that those under attack in the streets are the children of the very war martyrs who ensured the existence of the government that is now responsible for repressing them. Others besides grassroots activists took up this argument. The cultural products of the opposition candidates made this point as well, indicating that the challenge to official state narratives about the war were broad and diverse and at times came from those affiliated with the power structure.

The campaign materials of the main 2009 opposition candidates Karroubi and Mousavi, for example, went to great lengths to claim affiliation with both the revolution and the Iran-Iraq war. This was particularly the case in campaign films that were first broadcast on state television and later were circulated on sites such as YouTube. In the aftermath of the election, official sites linked to the opposition continued to stress their connections with the war martyrs, often pointing to the government's ill-treatment of the families of well-known martyrs. Numerous clips uploaded by official and independent supporters of the Green Movement exposed the government's hypocrisy in this regard. Although all such uses of the war were subject to interrogation in the comments sections, a line has been decidedly crossed as a result of the bold repurposing of material originally produced in relation to the war. Even videos uploaded with the apparent intent of keeping the songs and memories of war martyrs alive have been subject to reevaluation in relation to the events following 2009, and comments often disrupt official narratives of the eight-year conflict by accusing the government of debasing the memory and sacrifices of the war martyrs.

CONCLUSION

The Iranian state's massive investment in cultural products related to the eight-year war began soon after the Iraqi invasion and flourished throughout the bloody conflict. Since the end of hostilities in 1988, the war has continued to figure centrally in both state and nonstate constructions of national and political identity. More than twenty years after the end of the conflict, city murals honoring the war dead may have faded, but the government's desire to use the war and the public's appetite for war-themed materials have not. Popular films, best-selling books, and hundreds of Web sites related to the war are evidence of its continued resonance for diverse audiences. The capacity to digitally distribute audiovisual and other materials online has increased the recirculation of these materials, making it possible for state-sponsored films and videos to reach broader audiences.

This expansion has not been straightforward in its consequences for official narratives about the war and its legacy. The circulation of audiovisual material on global platforms such as YouTube has significantly changed the terrain. State-sponsored films and songs are available for use and reuse by populations the government could only dream of reaching in previous eras, including foreigners who translate and further distribute the material. Yet the state no longer controls how that material is framed and received. Even video clips posted by those who support official accounts are often challenged and remixed by an active audience. Users who repurpose state-endorsed content can undermine official narratives: footage that includes images of war alongside images of state repression of the opposition attacks core components of the state's official vision of itself during and after the war.

These conditions pose a conundrum for those in state power in Iran. As they continue to use the war to assert their narratives of contemporary events, they attempt to control conditions of production and reception so as not to expose the war to other interpretations. At the same time, they recognize the potential a virtual arm of its activities creates. State and state-supported institutions with an online presence offer carefully crafted narratives about the war and its legacy, but material posted to globally popular Web sites such as YouTube becomes subject to unpredictable and uncontainable contexts of interpretation. Thus, the ruling structure finds itself in the familiar but uncomfortable position of using a dual tactic of both restricting Internet activism and developing an Internet presence for its own purposes.

The government's investment in online venues for magnifying its reach must be read as part of the broader trend of state involvement online: the state has demonstrated increasing recognition of the fact that the virtual landscape is a contested one and that it must take steps to establish a foothold in that venue. With the rise of social media and its successful uses by the opposition following the June 2009 election, the state has become more explicit and militant in its commitment to maximizing the opportunities offered by digital technologies. The explosion in online materials about the war is testament to the diversity of the Iranian Internet. The following chapter considers this diversity with a focus on the rise of social media and examines the most explicit step the state has taken in making its mark online.

CHAPTER 4

SOCIAL MEDIA
AND THE MESSAGE

While the blogosphere dominated the Iranian Internet in the early years of the new millennium, the end of its first decade belonged to social media. Even more celebrated than Weblogistan, the term "social media" became the newest signifier of the liberatory potential of digital media. While the blogosphere had not met all of the potential attributed to it, social media seemed poised to surpass expectations. The social media mobilization that took place in the wake of the disputed Iranian election of 2009 seemed to confirm—at least for a short while—optimistic readings of the new technology as a "Twitter Revolution." In addition, the two Arab revolutions that succeeded less than two years after the Iranian demonstrations, one in Egypt and one in Tunisia, continued to sustain hopes about the transformative power of digital technologies. As in past periods, however, the Iranian Internet was a site of contestation as state actors and supporters of the state took up the same tools as their political opponents and critics. In fact, the state's stance toward media and cultural production became more aggressive in the era of social media.

The state's engagement with Internet media during this period became more explicit, especially in its campaign to confront and carry out a "soft war." These years are notable for the innovative and promising ways nonstate actors used digital media. The most widely celebrated instances of this relate to the aftermath of the 2009 election. As demonstrations unfolded, journalists and commentators hailed Iran's "Twitter Revolution" and credited it as the source of "riveting and thrilling reporting."[1] Others dubbed Twitter the "medium of the

83

movement" for its role in efforts to define and organize the protests.[2] In apparent recognition of Twitter's power, the U.S. Department of State asked the company to delay scheduled maintenance so that access to the service would not be disrupted as Iranians took to the street.[3] In addition to the great volume of journalistic analysis on the uses of social media during the demonstrations, scholarly commentaries on the topic have appeared as well (Khonsari, Nayeri, Fathalian, and Fathalian 2010; Rahimi 2011a, 2011b).

Once it became clear that demonstrators could not force the government's hand, no matter how cleverly they used the Internet, claims about the power of digital media during the fallout after the election became somewhat tempered. For example, technology enthusiast Clay Shirkey conceded that although "activists used every possible technological coordinating tool to protest," this was not enough to withstand the violence of the state (Shirkey 2011). Yet the sense remained that something remarkable had happened in the days after the disputed presidential election. And indeed, while the Iranian protesters did not succeed in having their demands met as their counterparts in the Arab world would go on to do in 2011 and thereafter, social media facilitated the rapid sharing of information, allowing opposition members to circumvent state restrictions on media and achieve widespread transnational solidarity.

Although the use of social media after the 2009 vote is a hallmark example of using digital media to resist the state in Iran, this focus has obscured important developments that appeared earlier, including those that emerged before the election. During the campaign period, social media made it possible for activists to create transnational and translocal spaces that at times seemed to approach an ideal public sphere. Users introduced and expanded new practices that relied on preexisting and emerging media, and a plurality of voices exchanged views in shared spaces. Innovations in the use of social media also led to the emergence of new communities of interpretation that played a central role in influencing discourses about the election. These promising uses of social media throughout the campaign period were not free of troubling aspects, but they deserve a more thorough assessment, especially in light of the fact that they have been almost completely overshadowed by the prominence of social media in accounts of the post-election period.

Throughout this period, state actors and their supporters also took advantage of social media. In keeping with its pattern of increasing involvement with digital media, the state continued to both suppress individual citizens' use of social media and engage with this new media proactively. The political crisis of the demonstrations after the elections, arguably the biggest the state had faced since its inception, and the central role it attributed to social media in its challenge to the ruling establishment motivated the state to revamp its approach to the media landscape. Although the state's new mode of involvement took shape in response to increased use of social media, it moved beyond that platform. As in all phases of the state's engagement with digital media, it was able to harness the full force of its resources and use existing media platforms. This period is distinguished by the state's attempts to lay out the parameters of its approach and to openly articulate how its political and cultural projects online and off are interlinked.

This chapter begins with an overview of the rise of social media, pinpointing factors and debates that shaped how it was used in the Iranian context. A close examination of two key moments in the surge of social media follows. The first moment is the presidential campaign period of 2009, a time when engagements with social media held much promise. The chapter focuses on the wildly popular Web site Friendfeed during the campaign period and highlights how the service made possible new modes of media practices, new kinds of social and political exchanges, and, for fleeting moments, the emergence of near-ideal public spheres. The chapter then moves to a consideration of the state's implementation of a strategy to confront mediated attacks on Iran's culture and values and to use the media to carry out its own assaults against its perceived enemies, a strategy it called the soft war.

SOCIAL MEDIA ON THE RISE

While there was no doubt about the popularity and power of social media sites after the 2009 presidential election, the shift toward new modes of engagement online was evident several years before that time. Like trends elsewhere, such as in the United States, social networking sites had been popular among users in Iran for several years. By 2006, for example, Iranians were among the most active participants on the Google-owned social networking site Orkut, prompting government censors to completely block the site. According to Open Net Initiative's 2006–2007 study on Iran, Orkut and Myspace were among the sites the government blocked completely.[4] Internet filtering was not always consistent; some ISPs blocked particular Web sites that others did not. The fact that two social networking sites were among those the government singled out for total blackout is a testament to their awareness of social media's rising popularity and potential for challenging the state. In the same period, other social networking sites, including Yahoo 360, Flickr, YouTube, and Facebook, were finding eager audiences in Iran. Many of the popular social media users had established themselves online as bloggers, indicating that while new platforms were becoming dominant, continuity with the older forms of digital media persisted.

In 2006, the year that saw a spike in the popularity of Orkut among Iranian users, two engineers in the Diaspora created the Persian-language Web site Balatarin, which was similar in concept to the social news aggregators Digg and Reddit, which were founded in 2004 and 2005, respectively. Like these sites, Balatarin depends on community participation.[5] Registered users submit items and links, and the fate of the submitted link depends on how fellow users vote. An item can become "hot" and rise to the top of a page or be eliminated altogether. It is the community of users, in short, that determines whether the item is worthy of attention or if it is so problematic that it should be removed.

In optimistic readings, such instances create democratic spaces and mobilize collective intelligence. Henry Jenkins is the most well-known proponent of this view. Borrowing from Pierre Levy, Jenkins points out the ability of online communities to "leverage the combined expertise of their members" (Jenkins 2006, 27). At the other end of the spectrum, critics of sites that rely on user participation have pointed out their tendency to encourage "hive mentality" (Lanier 2006) and the "tyranny of the minority" (Lerman 2007).

The relatively quick ascent of Balatarin was indicative of changes to come on the Iranian Internet: it foretold the popularity of social media and presaged both its power and it ugliness. In its self-description, Balatarin claims to have captured the best aspects of the participatory Web and avoided its pitfalls. In an update to the site's "About Us" section after the June 2009 election, Balatarin asserted that it was "the most popular Web 2.0 Web site in Persian," that it "played a crucial role in Iran's pro-democracy movement," and that it has an "unique point (credibility) system that prevents it from running into problems that similar Web sites such as digg.com have run into."[6] However, Balatarin's tendencies toward "mob rule" have often been the subject of criticism on the Iranian Internet. While it has functioned as a clearinghouse for breaking news, there is no doubt that readers used the site to advance political agendas. Its founders and many of its most avid participants are members of the Diaspora, a fact that would become significant as social media moved to constitute a dominant share of political activities on the Iranian Internet.

Another definitive marker of the shift to social media was apparent in the Iranian Internet's embrace of Google Reader. The platform, which was introduced in late 2005, became well known among Persian-language users in less than a year. Google Reader allows participants to customize news feeds through subscriptions. The opportunity it provided to access Web sites that at the time were filtered in Iran made it particularly attractive for Iranian users. Google Reader also offered a social component through its sharing and following features, which enabled users to construct networks for sharing information.

In 2009, Google Reader introduced commenting features, significantly enhancing the ability of users to interact about shared items.[7] By this time, Google Reader—which Iranians referred to by the composite moniker Gooder—was a well-established part of the Iranian Internet. The active presence of popular bloggers on Google Reader and their eventual use of the site to produce original content in addition to sharing existing links indicated an increasing shift away from traditional Web sites and blogs and a movement toward sites with advanced social networking capacities. When Google decided to disable Google Reader's social networking features, Iranian users protested loudly. While most of the Iranian outrage and disappointment over the impending demise of Google Reader was in Persian, the community of users eventually made enough noise to catch the attention of mainstream technology and news publications in the United States. Such accounts highlighted the usefulness of Gooder for evading censorship and credited Iranians with leading efforts to convince Google to reverse its decision.[8] At least one book intended for a popular audience has been published on the richness of Google Reader as a site for cultural investigation (Jami 2012).

While Gooder has received its share of recognition for the important role it played on the Iranian Internet, the social media site Friendfeed—which was at least as popular as Gooder, especially among users based in Iran—has not been adequately addressed. Friendfeed allows participants to incorporate feeds from other sites such as Facebook, Blogspot, Flickr, YouTube, and Twitter. Because of the Iranian government's filtering of Web sites, the ability of Iranians to go through multiple sites where users can post to a public forum is no small benefit and goes a long way toward explaining the popularity of Gooder and Friendfeed among Iranian users. In addition to having the option of automatically reproducing material they have already shared elsewhere, users can directly post to the site via e-mail or instant messenger services, providing another detour around governmental restrictions on access: In other words, users could still post information to the site even if they could not directly access it. In contrast to the user capabilities on Twitter and Facebook, Friendfeed users could edit their own posts after they had been shared on the site.[9] Users, including the author of a particular feed, may use the "like" or commenting functions to keep a post active (feeds that receive a "like" or a comment rise to the top of the page).[10] Friendfeed thus provides opportunities for both real-time and asynchronous communications. In addition, Friendfeed allows users to make private or public "rooms" where participants interested in a topic, theme, or project can gather. Finally, Friendfeed's restrictions on characters per feed are slightly higher than Twitter's limit of 140, and users can include hyperlinks within any given feed.

All of these factors figured into the popularity of the service with Iranian users, and the reasons for its exclusion from most assessments of social media in Iran are not clear. Much of the non-Persian-language commentary on the uses of social media in Iran and in the region has focused on Facebook and Twitter, sites that are also popular in North

America and Europe, where most of this commentary originates. This may explain why social media analysts outside Iran were predisposed to discuss Facebook and Twitter rather than Friendfeed and Google Reader, which did not catch on with North American and European audiences. Although some assessments included Friendfeed in the context of the emergence of the state's campaign against what it called a digital soft war, none paid any significant attention to Friendfeed's role in the campaign period. During that brief but intense period, Friendfeed illustrated both the realization and the dashing of the hopes that have accompanied the Internet since its inception.

SOCIAL MEDIA ON THE CAMPAIGN TRAIL

For approximately two months before Iran's explosive 2009 presidential election, the spaces created by the social networking aggregate service Friendfeed often seemed to approach an ideal public sphere. It made transnational and translocal participation from across the political spectrum possible. On this social media site, users whose geographical, social, or ideological locations would have prevented them from ever meeting or engaging with one another found a place to debate the most sensitive issues of the day in real time. The shared spaces where these discussions occurred transcended the social and political splits among camps. In ordinary offline circumstances, these groups would have had few opportunities for extensive contact. This is not to say that no such conversations took place on the ground, but Friendfeed combined the immediacy of face-to-face interactions with the shield of virtual distance, providing a relatively safe space for crossing boundaries and exchanging ideas.

Once the results of the election came in, however, the anger, fear, and distrust that spilled onto Iran's streets immediately became evident online. Many members of the site blocked their opponents, disabled public access to feeds, erased accounts, and/or created new, restricted accounts. The once-bustling arena of inclusive public discussion was effectively fragmented into small echo chambers.[11]

Despite the eventual disintegration of public spaces on Friendfeed, the campaign period was remarkable because of the innovative ways users combined emerging and preexisting forms of media. Complex new media practices emerged that seemed to bolster lively conversations, facilitate translocal and transnational exchange, and maximize the reach of networks. Some of the best examples of the new online behaviors relate to how individuals used Friendfeed to support their preferred candidates.

Like other social media sites, Friendfeed was particularly well suited for the dissemination of brief and pithy messaging, whether in verbal or visual form. Users took full advantage of such features to promote their candidates. According to online lore, in the second week of May, a fan of opposition candidate Mir-Hossein Mousavi shaded his Facebook profile picture with a green hue, urging all of his supporters to do the same. The idea almost immediately spread to other sites, most notably Friendfeed, and dozens of users tinted their avatars with a bright green. The rapid spread of the color on and offline initiated exchanges that illustrate how Friendfeed was functioning as a unique hub for debate across ideological lines.

When green first appeared as the symbol of the Mousavi campaign, no explicit explanation was given for the color choice. However, the cultural significance of green as the color of Islam and, in Iran, the color associated with those identified as direct descendants of the prophet (seyyeds), such as Mousavi, soon led to speculations about the motives for choosing that particular shade of green.

On May 21, Iran-based Friendfeed user Ahestan, who was already well known as the author of a blog of the same name and as a critic of reformists, asked Mousavi supporters to explain the meaning of the color green as a campaign symbol.[12] A Mousavi fan named Exir responded that Mir-Hossein Mousavi's supporters chose the color because he was a seyyed and green is the sign of seyyeds. In response, detractors criticized the move as an inappropriate capitalization on Mousavi's religious status. Supporters of Ahmadinejad, who was often accused of populism, were particularly adamant that Mousavi and his camp were guilty of the same. On the face of it, these exchanges may not seem particularly significant, but they are in fact quite remarkable, especially when one considers that within twenty-four hours of the election, it was difficult to find members of rival camps inhabiting the same virtual space, much less engaging each other with relative civility.

Members of the opposition were not the only ones whose symbols and discourses came under attack. Less than two weeks after
Friendfeed began turning green, campaigners for Ahmadinejad began
replacing their avatars with the national flag, even though they had
earlier mocked Mousavi supporters for adopting uniform symbols.[13]
In a clear jab at their green opponents, Ahmadinejad supporters
voiced the sentiment that "the color of the Ahmadinejad campaign
is green, white, and red because we don't want our country separated
into different colors."[14] Having adopted the flag as their symbol, however, it was now they who were subject to attack and interrogation.
Hamidreza—another blogger and active Friendfeed user—issued an
open appeal: "I am asking my friends not to allow Ahmadinejad supporters to co-opt the flag; make use of the flag in all Mousavi gatherings."[15] He also claimed that Ahmadinejad was not patriotic enough to
adopt the flag as his symbol.[16]

Others claimed that the flag belonged to all Iranians and temporar-
ily adopted it as their avatar, neither endorsing nor explicitly rejecting
the person of Ahmadinejad. One such user simply declared, "I put
up the Iranian flag, but not as a sign of Ahmadinejad," while another
noted, "[I am putting up] this flag of Iran so that our friends who
support Ahmadinejad know that Iran does not belong only to them
and our hearts too beat for Iran."[17]

Swiftly changing avatars and debates about the values and symbols of candidates illustrate how Friendfeed served as an extension of
political campaigns in Iran. The avatars, virtual equivalents of political buttons, functioned to signal party lines, foreshadowing the deep
splits that would ensue online and off after the disputed election. The
adoption of campaign signs and symbols made divisions visible that
had not been previously apparent, but they also stimulated conversations across the political spectrum.

Changing avatars was only one of many political meaning-making
gestures that took place on Friendfeed in the service of political campaigns. Some members used the site as a place to post photos of Iranians in order to make implicit claims about particular candidates.
For example, Ahmadinejad supporters circulated photos of fashion-
able young men and women with coifed hair (often dyed blond in the
case of women) who showed no outward signs of religiosity and were

Figure 13. This public Friendfeed post by an Ahmadinejad supporter uses images of trendy youth from a campaign event for Ahmadinejad.

openly carrying signs or symbols associated with the Ahmadinejad campaign.[18] These trends continued after the election; Ahmadinejad supporters shared photos of trendy youth attending pro-Ahmadinejad events and/or carrying placards indicating their sympathy with him or causes he supports. In such cases, the desire to show one's candidate as appealing to diverse groups overrode worries about codes of conduct and dress that concerned many of Ahmadinejad's socially conservative supporters.

Social media users who counted themselves among the opposition were not silent about the online distribution of such images. User Aghanader gol reposted one such photograph, which showed two young women flashing the victory sign while one held a poster of Ahmadinejad. The women wore heavy makeup, they had manicured nails, and they both had highlighted hair that flowed from beneath their scarves. Without the picture of Ahmadinejad, they personified the stereotype of the opposition and defied the codes of dress (hair fully covered, modest outfit and behavior) that religious Ahmadinejad supporters hold dear and in many cases demand that others follow. Pointing to this apparent hypocrisy, Aghanader gol addressed an

Ahmadinejad supporter and Friendfeed user by name: "Mohammad Hamed Eshanbakhsh, my dear brother, we are not saying that these people don't have a right to support Ahmadinejad. God willing they will increase in size. But the question remains, does Islam only become endangered with the hair of Mousavi and Karroubi supporters? How come you guys aren't screaming now about Islam? Because we not only accept such supporters with open arms, but as our friend Jalal would say, we would ask them: Are you single?"[19]

The question Aghanader gol asked was a serious one that exposed the double standard of the other camp, but the tone is playful, funny, and even flirtatious. One commenter angrily responded that he was disgusted with all of the hypocrisy, but most who contributed maintained the general tone of the original post. The user to whom the post was addressed defended himself by saying that he had no objection to the fact that candidates drew support from diverse groups. Rather, he claimed, he had a problem with the tactics the opposition was using to draw hip, young crowds. Although the discussions reached no resolution, the post is an example of Friendfeed at its pre-election best: controversial issues related to identity (of campaigns and of Iranian society at large) were broached directly and drew the participation of individuals from a range of views and backgrounds.

A third way that Friendfeed was mobilized during the campaign involves the relationship between the online service and television. For the first time in the history of Iran, the campaign for the presidency included live televised debates between all presidential candidates. The debates took place in pairs, so that each candidate had the chance to face every other candidate in a total of six televised events. The first debate, between reformist cleric Mehdi Karroubi and Mohsen Rezaei, the former head of the Revolutionary Guard, took place with relatively little instantaneous interaction on Friendfeed.[20] While many users later provided analysis of this debate or provided links to other sites that did so, only a few commented on it in real time.

This contrasts with the responses to debates featuring Ahmadinejad and reformist opposition candidates. These debates elicited torrential outpourings of instant commentary on Friendfeed and clearly demonstrated new modes of engaging with both the online user service and television. Multitasking users watched the debates while

Figure 14. This public Friendfeed post in support of reformist candidates
uses a photo circulated by the Ahmadinejad campaign to question the
hypocrisy of some of its tactics.

commenting on them in real time and interacting with others who
were doing the same. In essence, users transformed Friendfeed into
a transnational viewing community where participants from around
the world could act as both audience members and debate analysts.

Members of the Diaspora also participated in this new use of
media because they were able to watch the debates online or on satellite television stations. For those who did not have access to the
televised debates, Friendfeed acted as a live transcript, albeit one that
was accompanied with heated editorializing. Live commentators on
Friendfeed picked up on elements of the debates that would later
reverberate in other online and offline arenas. Thus, Friendfeed users
played a defining role in determining the issues that resonated and
would have a lasting impact on discourse.

In what would come to be known as one of the most controversial
moments of the debate, for example, Ahmadinejad objected to the

fact Mousavi had referred to former president Khatami as "Dr. Khatami," saying: "[My] ten minutes are over? I want to make one more statement. I just want to talk about the university degrees a little bit. You called Mr. Khatami 'doctor.' Do you know that one can only be called a doctor who has a doctoral degree from a university or has had a comprehensive [exam]? He has a bachelor's degree in philosophy, but you call him a doctor. Regarding the case of a lady, can I talk to you about the educational record of a lady? Yes? Should I say it? No, should I say it? Are you sure?"[21]

The "lady" to whom Ahmadinejad referred was Mousavi's wife, Zahra Rahnavard, an artist, academic, and former head of Alzahra University in Tehran. Because Rahnavard received her PhD during the Cultural Revolution (1980–1987) that resulted in the temporary closing and purging of the universities, Ahmadinejad was insinuating that Rahnavard's degree was the result of political nepotism. More shockingly, his accusation was also a thinly veiled attack on key developments in the postrevolution period.

Large segments of the Friendfeed audience, however, were not interested in the implications of Ahmadinejad's statement for assessing the Cultural Revolution. Instead, they immediately reacted to this barely disguised accusation against the opposition candidate's wife, angrily echoing sentiments that "he had done the ugliest thing possible"[22] and that he had crossed a line by attacking "the honor"—that is to say, the woman— of his rival. The gendered components of the massive response to Ahmadinejad's remarks merit a separate analysis that is outside the scope of the considerations here. Suffice it to say that discourses of the period often revealed underlying tensions about questions of gender. In this case, groups that openly advocated equality between men and women as part of their political goals resorted to the gendered logic of "honor" and protection in critiquing their opponents. While some users pointed to such tensions, anger at Ahmadinejad for his perceived transgression dominated the on-the-spot reactions. The debate, particularly the segment with Ahmadinejad's attack on Zahra Rahnavard, would be later critiqued in a number of other old and new media forums. Friendfeed users, however, were among the first, if not *the* first, to hone in on and highlight the exchange in public or semi-public forums.

In addition to allowing users to identify key issues and preserve moments from the live debates, Friendfeed enabled users to make a case about who won the debates as they were unfolding on state television. This is another example of how conversations took place on Friendfeed across previously impermeable lines in the pre-election period, providing rare evidence of the complexities of the social and political landscape in Iran. Even fights over candidates and their agendas during this time, bitter as they were becoming, showed promise because Friendfeed users were traversing geographical and ideological boundaries and approaching controversial issues more openly and for broader audiences than in previous election periods.

After the election, as anger and frustration over the results mounted to dangerous levels, Friendfeed collapsed. Many users blocked their perceived political opponents from participating on their pages, made their accounts private, or deleted their accounts altogether. The archives that remain from the pre-election days are therefore all the more valuable: they provide glimpses into a unique historical moment that is as important for what it reveals about the complexities of contemporary Iranian society as it is for what it reflects about the role of new media. In the pre-election period, Friendfeed facilitated the coming together of multiple platforms from new and traditional media sources and provided a glimpse of the exciting possibilities of media convergence.

Soft War on the Iranian Internet

Friendfeed and other bustling online gathering places were not the only sites to experience radical change in the wake of the Iranian election. Major shifts also became evident in the state's activities and in its approaches to social media and the Internet. In the periods covered in previous chapters, the state's approach to digital media was two pronged: a repressive arm filtered content and controlled Internet speed and a cultural arm produced content and participated online. These complementary but largely separate modes of responding to digital media seemed to merge in the aftermath of the election as part of the state's strategy to both wage and fight a "soft war." This strategy aimed to subvert what the state claimed were media-based assaults on Iranian values and culture by educating the public about the perceived enemy's media tactics and producing competing media content. While official formulations of "soft war" addressed a range of media, they placed particular emphasis on Internet technologies. Various forms of social media had taken root on the Iranian Internet several years before the Iranian state faced the massive post-election protests. The state had become aware that user trends were moving in this direction and had adjusted its two-pronged approach accordingly. It fine-tuned blocking mechanisms to slow the flow of traffic on social media sites. At the same time, state-sanctioned Web sites, state organizations, and state officials were establishing a presence in the very spaces that censors often filtered. In short, while the ruling powers may have been taken aback by the hundreds of thousands who took to the street to protest the election results, they had been aware for several years of the potential of social media to challenge state power. In fact, when protesters hit the streets in June 2009, arrest warrants for some activists explicitly referred to their social media participation (Ziyaee-Parvar 2009).

Despite the state's awareness of the shifting terrain online and its attempts to confront potential threats, the intersection of massive demonstrations and the use of digital media seems to have created a large enough shock to the ruling system to necessitate a change in official responses. Because of the significant role members of the Diaspora and sympathetic international and state-owned media outside Iran played in magnifying the events that unfolded in the streets, the state identified the enemy as both internal and external and it realized that participants on both sides of the country's borders were talking to each other. In November 2009, for example, only a few months after the presidential election, Supreme Leader Ayatollah Khamenei said in a speech to his supporters: "Today, the country's top priority is to fight against the enemy's soft war."[23] Soon thereafter, this direct quote or some version of it was repeated by a range of figures in Iran's complex ruling establishment.[24] Significantly, the quote was cited as the impetus for the establishment of projects dedicated to fighting against soft war, and many official blogs and Web sites devoted to heeding the Leader's call to action prominently displayed Khamenei's statement.[25] The speech continues to reverberate in the noninstitutionalized sites of the Internet as well, where individuals who support the government identify with the campaign to fight against and wage a soft war.

Discussions of "soft" threats had cropped up in official discourses in Iran over the decade before the 2009 protests. These discussions often identified a range of media outlets as the bases from which cultural and political attacks on Iran were launched. It is true that generous funding from foreign states in the first decade of the new millennium had led to a proliferation of Persian-language media that targeted an Iranian audience and promoted political agendas against the ruling powers in Iran. Because these outlets include an online component or conduct their entire enterprise virtually, the Iranian state attempted to respond to the threat they posed both online and in other ways. State media platforms targeted foreign-funded media in official discourses, and the state filtered the content of Web sites of those who opposed it and disrupted satellite broadcasts that criticized the Iranian government.

Yet while there is continuity in state rhetoric and the state's responses to digital technologies, the period after the 2009 protests is distinguished by the state's discourses and policies about what it calls "soft war." Unlike "hard" forms of war, such as conventional warfare or other forms of militarized operations, soft war is not overtly coercive or destructive. Rather, it aims to seduce the target society to share the values and beliefs of those carrying out the soft war. In this regard, what the Iranian state has called "soft war" is similar to Joseph Nye's definition of "soft power." Although states may use their economic or military power (i.e., hard power) to force the hands of their opponents, they can also persuade them by showcasing the attractiveness of the particular state's way of life and values (Nye 2009). Echoing Iranian officials' claims about the effect of foreign organizations and media, Nye has identified a country's cultural and policy institutions as vehicles for exercising soft power against other societies.[26] To make matters more confusing, Iranian discourses on the tactics of perceived enemies sometimes use the term "soft war" interchangeably with "soft power."

Although what is called soft war in Iran is about soft power, it is also distinct from it. In other words, while its main concerns are about the use of soft power against Iranian culture and values, soft war encompasses a broader concept and set of discourses.[27] As a strategy, soft war marks a new phase that unifies the repressive and proactive approaches of the state to digital media. Whereas in the past the state's aggressive rhetoric about fighting foreign cultural invasion and the repressive tactics used to prevent it (filtering content, slowing down the Internet, etc.) operated alongside its proactive attempts to produce media content, the soft war phase emphasizes the overlaps in the two: producing material and fighting material produced by the enemy are integrated. In addition, the state linked online communication and offline events more closely than it had done in the past, expanding its efforts to take advantage of the convergence of spaces that had allowed the opposition to magnify its reach.

The state's soft war phase has been implemented in several overlapping ways. To begin with, there has been a veritable media explosion in Iran about the concept of soft war. Numerous newspaper articles, books, and television programs appeared with the goal of informing the Iranian public about the soft war the enemy was waging and how to respond. This includes mobilizing state actors and individuals to produce media content and analysis that attracts new audiences and undermines the enemy's soft war. In other words, part of fighting against the enemy's soft war is waging the state's own version in response.[28] For example, on August 22, 2011, during a television show on soft war (discussed below), the deputy director of the Center for Digital Media of the Ministry of Culture and Islamic Guidance emphasized that participation in the soft war should not just be defensive: "It is not necessary for us to only be defending in this war, we can also attack. We must be attentive to all the opportunities that are available to us internationally and not wait around until we are attacked. We must have appropriate defensive and offensive policies."[29] State organs openly promised financial backing for publications and cultural productions on the issue. In November 2011, for example, the deputy minister of culture and Islamic guidance said that providing support for works about the soft war was one of the ministry's top priorities.[30]

Much of the material that circulated in books and traditional media was reviewed by authors of Web sites that self-identified as participants in the soft war. Similarly, blog posts and other online activities that participated in the state's call to respond to the soft war from foreign states and from Iranians opposed to the government in power interacted with offline media. The Web site of Dabir Khane Daemei Moqabele ba Jang-e Narm-e Keshvar (The Country's Permanent Secretariat for Confronting Soft War), for example, contains many articles that are also found in the hardline newspaper *Kayhan* (which also carries the articles on its own Web site). This interlinking of digital and traditional media spaces in the service of responding to the soft war can also be seen in the actions of individuals. Like their counterparts in the opposition, those who support the state have created a culture of Internet specialists and celebrities. The emergence of the soft war phase has provided new opportunities for such individuals. For example, on August 22, 2011, some of these experts appeared on an episode of the television show *Raz* entitled "The Dos and Don'ts of Cyberspace." The main discussion focused on social media as a space where soft war is carried out against Iran and how Iranian "soldiers of soft war" can confront and respond to the perceived threats.

None of the participants in the roundtable questioned the importance of the soft war strategy, but their discussions revealed the internal inconsistencies and disagreements about soft war and digital policy more broadly. For example, the only cleric participating in the debate, Hamidreza Gharibreza, the head of an institution devoted to religious dialogue who also has an active personal website, questioned the policy of filtering Facebook and noted that blocking the site amounted to "taking away the weapons from our Soft Warriors."[31] Mohammad Saleh Meftah, who is very active on social media and writes for the hardline Web site Teribon, similarly complained about the "double standards" in the state's stance toward digital media because it undermines the ability of state supporters to participate in the soft war.[32] In short, inconsistencies in the state's media policies and the exact parameters of soft war puzzle even the state's ardent supporters.

Despite internal disputes about state policy, the episode of *Raz* shows that the state and its supporters are able to harness the power of both new and traditional media to promote their ideas about digital media policy and soft war. After airing on national television, the episode was made available for streaming on the show's Web site and various news and analysis Web sites.[33] Unlike critics of the state who are generally limited to digital media for disseminating their views, state organs have the means to deploy the full force of interlinked media spaces to maximize their reach, and the state's access to funds and media outlets and a range of traditional media give it an advantage in the number of media forms it is able to mobilize.

The connectivity and constant flow between virtual content and what takes place offline may give the sense that there is a dead-end circularity to the state-promoted strategy of fighting and waging a soft war. The proliferation of publications about the soft war appears to be part of the strategy itself. Indeed, much of the discourse about the issue stresses the importance of raising public awareness of and education about how to resist soft war tactics from abroad. The educational component is most clearly reflected in August 2011 comments by the country's minister of education, who announced the ministry's intention to make "fundamental changes to [K–12] textbooks" in order to "confront the threat of soft war" by "inoculating" youth.[34]

Another clear indication that knowledge production about the soft war is understood to be a core component of combating and engaging in soft war can be seen on the Web site Jang-e Narm:

Figure 15. The Web site of Iran's Secretariat for Confronting Soft War.

Akhareen Akhbar va Etelaat-e Hozey-e Amaliyat-e Ravani va Jang-e
Narm [Soft war: The latest news and information in the field of psychological operations and soft war]. The Web site is not transparent
about who owns or funds it, but its affinity with hardline elements
of the state is clear from its rhetoric and frequent references to the
Supreme Leader. This site closely links psychological operations with
soft war and uses the abbreviation for the former as its URL (psyop.
ir). It defines soft war as a wide range of "cultural, literary, artistic,
propaganda, linguistic, and communication" practices that aim to
change a society's "way of thought." Its "About Us" section calls psychological operations a "major agent of soft war" and identifies raising awareness about the soft war as its "critical cultural mission." It
aims to fulfill this mission by informing its readers about new "books,
publications, articles, software as well as the latest news, reports, and
relevant developments in research on the issue [of soft war]."[35] It is
clear that producing and circulating information—online and off—
about the "enemy's soft war" is central to the stated aim of protecting
the people from its onslaught.

Jang-e Narm emphasizes that new strategies are being used against
Iran that require new responses. A November 2011 piece on the site
covering Ayatollah Khamenei's warnings about a "cultural invasion"
begins with the following epigraph from Khamenei's speech: "My

Figure 16. The Soft War Web site, whose URL is the perhaps telling psyop.ir.

dears, today the issue of a cultural invasion through the use of new technologies is very serious . . . they are using various methods via television, radio, and computers to dump massive amounts of various ideas. We must stand up to these things. Today, we cannot rely on our old methods."[36] Other articles such as "The Challenges and Strategies for Dealing with 'Cultural NATO'" similarly warn against new types of threats and the need to confront them in creative ways.[37] Since proponents of the strategy to fight and carry out soft war identify the Internet as a main site of danger, they stress that state supporters should keep abreast of the latest media technologies: "All capacities and the latest technologies must be used in getting [our] message across in this arena [of soft war]."[38]

Although Jang-e Narm analyzes a wide range of threats (which include everything from the entertainment-focused satellite channel Man-o-To and its popular talent show featuring Iranian diva Googoosh to Voice of America's Broadcasting Board of Governors to a range of Web sites it identifies as "anti-Iranian"), it shares with other participants in the soft war endeavor a tendency to slide between talking about soft war as an offensive strategy and talking about it as a defensive strategy. The lack of clarity about the parameters of soft war notwithstanding, the massive resources devoted to its explicit pursuit on the Iranian Internet and beyond reflect a shift from earlier state-sponsored and pro-state approaches to digital technologies. The state's campaign against the soft war eschewed the niceties of its previous reactions to digital communication when it complemented its repressive approaches with a range of tactics that sought to influence discourse on and about the Iranian Internet. Its calls for innovation open the door for the involvement of a wide range of participants, including various ministries and supporters of the ruling system. Both entities that are officially linked to the state and Web sites that support the state (which may or may not be state funded) have become more aggressive in the terms they use. The Web site Afsaran (Soldiers), for example, claims to be inspired by the Supreme Leader's statements about soft war.[39] The state itself has gone beyond using militarized language and has actively courted the military in its soft war efforts. For example, during a January 2013 government-sponsored conference on "Mobilizing Cyber Battalions," the deputy head of the joint armed forces announced that a headquarters for soft war would be established for the joint forces.[40] That institutions of hard war and state violence are integrating soft war into their establishments is a telling marker of the state's new media policy, where the repressive arm of the state is combined with the tactics it has used to produce media content.

CONCLUSION

The Iranian Internet has had a noisy transition into the second decade of the new millennium. The tumultuous events of 2009 revived celebratory analysis of the impact of digital media. Although the ruling structure survived the demonstrations and the support for the demonstrations outside the country that social media made possible, the sense among commentators and opposition movement members that the new technology had the potential to overthrow even the most entrenched powers endured. This faith in social media was enhanced in the wake of the successful Arab revolutions in Egypt and Tunisia in 2010–2011.

Yet for all the attention the post-election uprising and its aftermath have received, much has remained unexamined. If the days following the election were remarkable because of how protesters used social media to disseminate their message internally and outside Iran, this chapter has shown that the time before the vote was also noteworthy in a number of ways that have been overlooked. In the lead-up to the election, social media users pushed the boundaries of various modes of engaging with media and politics. This group became influential as they created new communities of interpretation. However, the pluralistic public spheres that emerged within the arena of social media could not withstand offline developments. The digital world may be well suited for traversing geographical and ideological boundaries, but sometimes events on the ground overcome the limits of the online world. In the immediate aftermath of the 2009 election, the massive demonstrations and the unleashing of repressive state power left very little space for nuances in positions, and many social media spaces retracted into gigantic echo chambers, where users limited their interactions to those with the same political views as themselves. Nonetheless, the campaign period remains noteworthy for the development of innovative uses of social media. Iranian users of the popular but often ignored social aggregator Friendfeed redefined media practices and found new ways to be politically active online. Dynamic social media sites of exchange such as Friendfeed may not have been able to sustain themselves in Iran after the election, but they are an important example of the realized potential of online engagement, even if the achievement was short lived in Iran.

On the Iranian Internet, the consequences of the post-election fallout went beyond the disintegration of previously dynamic spheres of exchange. Those in seats of power and policy makers responded to the crisis by openly articulating a new approach to old and new media landscapes. The launch of the state's response to what it called a soft war signaled a more aggressive stance that relied on mobilizing the state's vast resources for producing and disseminating information. While state apparatuses and officials have taken an active role in relation to the Iranian Internet since its early days, the advent of the soft war era brought notable changes in how this role has been formulated and carried out. The Iranian state recognizes that social media has been instrumental in blurring the increasingly permeable boundaries between traditional and digital media, and its approach evolved to become at once more holistic (by including multiple institutions and media platforms) and more aggressive (by formulating the terms of its strategy and integrating it with organs of state power such as the army).

Overall, the last years of the first decade of the new millennium were eventful even by the standards of Iran and the boisterous transnational networks of the Iranian Internet. As the decade came to a close, social media dominated over other forms of online engagement, a trend that had begun in 2006. The outcomes of the 2009 election and its aftermath were contradictory: innovative uses of digital media and the expansion of networks for exchange emerged alongside troubling uses of the same technologies by state and individual actors who support the state's agenda. As users began using social media more

intensively, the state adjusted its stance accordingly. While changes
in official responses to online technologies and user patterns has
been characteristic of the Iranian Internet since its earliest years, the
state's campaign against what it calls the soft war is an unprecedented
approach with consequences that are still unfolding.

CONCLUSION

New Media Futures

This book ends its examination three years after the Iranian Internet made a noisy transition into the second decade of the new millennium. At this moment, social media sites are still bustling; formerly thriving blogs have been erased or languish without updates, readers or comments; and many static Web sites from what in Internet years are long ago are completely unavailable or sit untouched, joining a long list of others on Internet ghost towns.

Examining the conditions of the Iranian Internet's conception and the trajectory of its development provides some clues about what the future might bring. The conflicted situation surrounding its infancy inside Iran, when state organs promoted the technology and enabled the telecommunications infrastructure at the same time that they devised the parameters for restricting it by filtering content and limiting speeds, set the stage for the state's active but often contradictory relationship with digital media. Outside the country, the embrace of the new medium within the Diaspora brought the promise of reconnecting with a lost homeland, but it often also provided evidence of the depth of the chasm between an imagined Iran and the real Iran.

The broader social and political contexts of the emergence of the Iranian Internet were also complex. For many, particularly young segments of the population in Iran, the victory of the reformists around the time the Internet became popular increased hope that a radically different era would arise from the intersection of new media and new politics. Outside Iran, the reaction to the reformists was less enthusiastic, and many who had left in the earliest years after the revolution

exhibited outright hostility to any politicians who came from within
the Islamic Republic's power structure. Yet even among those in the
Diaspora who rejected the reformists or viewed them with suspicion,
many placed hope in the new generation of politically and socially
active youth who were entering public arenas alongside the politicians
they had elected. This same generation was also beginning to find a
voice in the Diaspora. Unlike many of their parents or those who were
slightly older than themselves, they had the language skills and the
temerity to enter public debates about Iran in their adopted home-
lands. These dynamics among resident and Diasporic Iranians nour-
ished the new media spheres, presenting opportunities for clashes and
collaborations across generations, ideologies, and physical locations.

One result of the massive demonstrations after the 2009 presidential election was a resurgence of reformist candidates, politicians,
and theoreticians. Yet the revival was not able to withstand the heavy
hand of the ruling establishment. With leading figures under house
arrest and others reconciling with the powers that be, the political fate
of the reformists—and indeed, the possibilities for reform overall—
are at best uncertain. On the other end of the political spectrum, the
picture is also bleak. If Mahmoud Ahmadinejad was once the favored
candidate of the country's Supreme Leader, his political fortunes have
dimmed since 2009. In the four years since the last election, attacks
on his administration and advisors were a mainstay of discourses in
Iran's media and political spheres, and some of his closest advisors
faced investigation or arrest. The factionalism and realignments that
characterize contemporary Iranian politics continue unabated, but the
politics and alliances that have formed as a result are markedly different from the moments under consideration in the book's first chapters.

The downward spiral of Iran's economy must also be taken into
consideration when accounting for the changes on the Iranian Internet. Intensifying sanctions against Iran by the United States and the
European Union have led to high unemployment and inflation. These
sanctions have targeted the country's banking and oil industries.
The constant threats of war and additional embargoes have created
anxiety for those in power, who have responded by increasing social
and political restrictions. Increased economic and political pressures
have produced more emigrants, and new generations of Iranians are

joining their predecessors in Europe and North America, again changing the makeup of the Diaspora.

Radical changes in the international context are also important for understanding developments on the Iranian Internet this book describes. The most significant geopolitical change for Iran during this period was the U.S. intervention in the region that defeated the republic's most significant regional enemies. However, the new relationships Iran was able to establish in the region were accompanied by a strong U.S. presence in Afghanistan and Iraq. The resulting triangular dynamics among Iran, its neighbors, and the United States continued throughout the years this book covers. The increased role of the United States in the region under George W. Bush's presidency included a "soft power" component, and his administration and, later, Barack Obama's administration spent millions of dollars to "promote democracy" in Iran. Much of this funding was used to fortify and establish media outlets targeting audiences inside Iran. These funds have also gone to members of the Diaspora to run the dozens of magazines, news sites, and organizations that have appeared. The various responses of the Iranian state apparatus to these developments have been noted throughout the book and have culminated in its soft war strategy, which targets foreign-backed cultural products and political discourses online and off.

The surprise eruption of the "Arab Spring" was the next major event that had implications for understanding the past and future of the Iranian Internet. The first wave of revolutions in North Africa, which unfolded less than two years after the massive demonstrations in Iran in 2009, became the subject of much wrangling both online and off. Those in power and their supporters, many of whom dubbed the events an "Islamic Awakening," traced the revolutions in North Africa to the legacy of Iran's 1979 revolution. In contrast, the Iranian opposition, especially the Green Movement saw the revolutions as a manifestation of the same people's power that had poured into the streets of Iran in 2009 and expressed solidarity with the aim of overthrowing dictators. As more Arab countries have witnessed their version of the Arab Spring, skirmishes over claiming and interpreting changes have continued on the Iranian Internet, becoming another locus where the nature of the Iranian state and society are contested.

At the time of this writing, much remains unresolved about recent changes in the region. In the countries that ignited the Arab Spring, Tunisia and Egypt, struggles over political and personal rights continue. The NATO bombings of Libya disrupted narratives of people's uprisings, and foreign interference in other countries such as Bahrain and Syria have turned those countries into proxy sites for hashing out bigger geopolitical struggles. In short, the nonviolent protests of the Arab Spring have in some cases turned to armed and violent conflicts, and a heavy price has been paid in terms of human life and suffering. Given these complexities, the appetite for claiming and contesting the Arab Spring on the Iranian Internet has waned. Nonetheless, the uncertainty about what the future holds for Iran's neighboring states continues to generate a nervous energy about the consequences for Iran's own political fortunes.

This book has shown how the Iranian Internet has flourished amid these developments. In the Internet's earliest days, members of the Diaspora who initially dominated because of technical reasons led the way in maximizing the full force of the new technology and organized transnational campaigns with results that satisfied participants. If the Internet was the vehicle for driving these campaigns, nationalism was the fuel. In other words, simply using the new medium was not enough to draw widespread cooperation. It is ironic that the glue of nationalist sentiment was necessary for the establishment of transnational connectivity. Mixed results—in this case innovative uses of digital media emerged at the same time as users relied on troubling constructions of communal belonging—most accurately describe what lay in store for participants on the Iranian Internet and their results, be they individual, independent, and/or state-linked actors.

If members of the Diaspora were the leaders in setting some of the parameters of Internet-based participation in the days of Web 1.0, the prolific posts of diverse bloggers writing in Persian expanded the virtual terrain enough to garner international attention. Many accounts of the Iranian blogosphere, which often cited statistics that showed that Persian at one time was the third most used language on the Web, celebrated secular and oppositional blogs for pushing boundaries and defying the ruling state. Yet fascinating aspects of Weblogistan are dismissed or elided in narrow frameworks that capture only those blogs that are antagonistic to Islam and/or the ruling structure in Iran. Some of the most critical commentaries on contemporary Iranian society and politics come from the diverse bloggers who do not fit this model, several of whom have been detained or harassed by Iranian authorities despite their explicit support for those in power. To see Weblogistan in its unwieldy totality—rather than in bits and pieces that fit a preconceived mold—is to begin to understand its complexities and the complexities of the offline spaces to which it is reciprocally related.

Alongside the expansion of blogs, the onset of the capacity for individuals to upload and share audiovisual materials brought new sets of possibilities on the Iranian Internet. This leveled the playing field somewhat, and organizations, states with resources, and tech-savvy individuals no longer had the advantage in terms of producing and circulating this content. Individual users began reframing or repurposing existing materials and circulating them to audiences worldwide that had previously been inaccessible. The opportunities for producing original materials also increased and proved particularly useful for activists who were disseminating materials that documented local unrest or human rights violations. Depending on their sensibilities and political agendas, participants broke political taboos or reaffirmed them as they reused, remixed, and produced audiovisual materials on the Iranian Internet.

Throughout these overlapping periods on the Iranian Internet—the days of static Web sites, the heyday of the blogosphere, the birth of sites where audiovisual materials could be uploaded, and the rise of social media—state power has been present. The state created and developed the infrastructure necessary for the Internet to function and develop in the 1990s, and since that time, state apparatuses have continuously fine-tuned a range of mechanisms for controlling access. The attempts of state entities to filter content, slow down Internet speed, and monitor the activities of dissidents, among other repressive tactics, have been well documented in the popular and academic literature on the relationship between Iran's ruling structure and emerging media.

The role of the state as an active participant online, on the other hand, has been rarely recognized or examined. As the previous chapters have highlighted, state powers have recognized the importance of using digital media and generating cultural products online and have actively engaged in both since the earliest days of the Iranian Internet. The result has been a range of activities, including projects that have sought to influence content produced on the Internet. Actors and institutions linked to the state have established strongholds on the Iranian Internet, in some cases even co-opting campaigns and discourses that originated with those who oppose the ruling establishment. Similarly, state institutions, which were initially able to dominate in the realm of online audiovisual content, digitized and uploaded a variety of materials that support official narratives about Iran's history and contemporary realities.

None of the state's attempts to entrench itself online have gone uncontested. This constitutes one of the most consistent and hopeful aspects of the Iranian Internet: individuals and organizations can undermine the state's claims to power and assertions of legitimacy as soon as they are made, using the same technologies and often in the same virtual locations. This, of course, has its downside, especially in cases of anonymous participation, where unkind, racist, sexist, and/or threatening speech can thrive without consequence. Although the fluidity of information and the multiplying spaces for its dissemination provide fertile ground for the growth of troubling tendencies, they also provide opportunities for pushing back against those tendencies.

Both the dashed hopes and the successes of diverse participants on the Iranian Internet provide lessons about assessing and participating in its dynamic landscapes. Looking back at the sixteen years examined in the previous chapters, from the Iranian Internet's genesis in the mid-1990s to its stormy transition into the second decade of the new millennium, this book concludes on an optimistic note. Because the difficulties of grasping the implications of rapidly developing digital technologies are compounded by the volatility of their contexts of reception among resident and Diasporic Iranians, any predictions about what the future holds would be imprudent. Nonetheless, hope remains that the Iranian Internet of the future might be characterized more by the innovations and interactions of independent users connecting across geographical and ideological divides than by the interventions of Iranian and foreign states attempting to use the Internet to engage in domestic and foreign power struggles.

NOTES

1. While there are some disagreements over the exact timing of the transition from Web 1.0 to Web 2.0, the former generally refers to the early years of the Web in the late 1990s, when the Web was characterized by static Web sites that offered few (if any) opportunities for user interactivity. In contrast, the Web in the new millennium has developed toward expanding such options. Everything from blogs to photo-sharing sites to social media has aimed at increasing user participation. Hence, Web 2.0 is often referred to as the participatory web.

2. Substantial U.S. and other state funding has been used to impact Iranians' experience with the Internet in two interrelated ways pertaining to access and to content accessed. The former has primarily taken the form of proxies, Virtual Public Network (VPN), and other anti-filtering software. Proxy servers provide users with an intermediary between their computers and the sites they are attempting to access. They hide or misidentify users' IP addresses, therefore providing a way to get around filters that deny access to Iran-based users. Virtual Private Network (VPN) software similarly has an IP-hiding function: user activity on Web sites will show the IP of the country of the VPN. Other software such as Ultrasurf and Freegate gives users access to a collection of proxies. In addition to funding development and training in the use of censorship-evading technologies, foreign funding has aimed at influencing Internet content that is available to Iranian audiences. To this end, a range of news and analysis sites have benefited from various forms of direct and indirect state funding. Roozonline and Radio Zamaneh, both funded by the Dutch, are two examples of this. In addition, the Persian services of state media such as Voice of America (VOA), Radio Farda, British Broadcasting Corporation (BBC), Deutsche Welle, and others have expanded their Web sites and their presence on the Internet more generally. Many writers and journalists working with such media are also active online, producing content both in their personal capacities and in their official positions, although the line between the two is not always clear. Finally, there is the issue of covert

113

funding for online activities, which is by definition difficult to trace or verify. As the following chapters will outline, the Iranian state has attempted to use similar tactics to influence Internet content and technologies. 3. Filtering is the Iranian state's main mechanism for controlling access to content online. In the late 1990s, private ISPs filtered content in inconsistent and haphazard ways on their own. In this period, users could get around filtering mechanisms by simply trying multiple ISPs. In 2001, when the government required all commercial ISPs to connect to the Internet via the state's telecommunications company, it set the stage for centralized control over the Internet. Also in 2001, a governmental decree by the Supreme Council of the Cultural Revolution required that all ISPs use filtering systems. Nonetheless, the orders for which content should be filtered and who could issue these orders have not been centralized.

1   REEMBODIED NATIONALISMS

1 For an overview of key debates in Diaspora studies during this period, see Braziel and Mannur (2003).

2 Gonzales and Rodriguez have attributed these hopeful assessments to the speed and ease with which information can be exchanged on digital media, noting that what they call the "democratic informationalism" of the Internet not only has the ability to bypass national boundaries but "claims to transcend and obliterate all borders—embodied, national, and global" (Gonzalez and Rodriguez 2003, 216).

3 Nicholas Negroponte, "Internet Is Way to World Peace," CNN Interactive, November 25, 1997, http://www.cnn.com/TECH/9711/25/internet.peace. reut/, quoted in Kluver (2001). Kluver's article challenges Negroponte's assertion about the Internet's ability to undermine nationalism.

4 Eriksen (2007) has identified five types of ways Web sites relate to nationalism: sponsorship by the state, as surrogates for the state, as expressions of pre-independence positions, as sites of multiculturalism, and in opposition to the state.

5 For an overview of developments in Iranian Internet technology from 1993 to 2001, see Rahimi (2003). For an account that considers issues of access during this period, see Johari (2002). For an account of infrastructural developments in Internet technologies during the 1990s in Iran and the broader Persian Gulf region, see Burkhart and Goodman (1998).

6 Phone interview with Foaad Khoshmood, chief technical officer of Iranian.com, August 2007.

7 Farhad Kashani, "Boycott KLM," Iranian.com, November 21, 1996, http://iranian.com/Dec96/Features/PersianGulf/PersianGulf.html#Boycott.

NOTES TO PAGES 19–23 115

8 "The Persian Gulf Debate," Iranian.com, December 1996, http://iranian.
com/Dec96/Features/PersianGulf/PersianGulf.html.
9 Examples of dissenting voices in this debate can be found at the following
URLs: Kambiz Kashani, "Chill Out," Iranian.com, http://iranian.com/Dec96/
Features/PersianGulf/PersianGulf.html#Chill; Abbas Soltani, "Molla Nasre-
din," Iranian.com, http://iranian.com/Dec96/Features/PersianGulf/Persian-
Gulf.html#Molla; and Laura Rosen, "Feed the Hungry," Iranian.com, http://
iranian.com/Dec96/Features/PersianGulf/PersianGulf.html#Hungry.
10 Some examples include "News and Views," Iranian.com, December
1998, http://iranian.com/News/Dec98/pg2.html; Bagher R. Harandi, "Tehran
to Tel Aviv," Iranian.com, January 7, 1999, http://iranian.com/Letters/Jan99/
index.html#72; Ali Nikseresht, "Not the Arabian or the Persian Gulf," January
7, 1999, Iranian.com, http://iranian.com/Letters/Jan99/index.html#71; A.R.
Begli Beigie, "Cultural Continuity: To Keep a Culture One Needs to Preserve
its Traditions," November 8, 2001, Iranian.com, http://iranian.com/ARBeg-
liBeigie/2001/November/PG/index.html; Amir. N, "Persian (Traitors) Gulf,"
November 29, 2004, Iranian.com, http://www.iranian.com/Opinion/2004/
November/PG/index.html; and Mahin Bahrami, "The illiterate Gulf," December 12, 2004, Iranian.com, http://iranian.com/MBahrami/2004/December/
PG/index.html.
11 Previously available at http://www.persiangulfonline.org/aboutus/Wha-
tIsPGO.htm.
12 Previously available at http://www.persiangulfonline.org/aboutus/
whereweare.htm.
13 Previously available at http://www.persiangulfonline.org/contactus.htm.
14 "About Us," Persian Gulf Taskforce, previously available at http://www.
persiangulfonline.org/aboutus/WhatIsPGO.htm.
15 Previously available at http://www.persiangulfdefense.com/ (accessed
August 2005). The quotations are taken from the "About Us" and "Core Values" sections of the site.
16 As soon as single-issue Web sites such as the Persian Gulf Defense Fund
site became defunct, other sites using similar rhetoric sprang up to take their
place. Persiangulf.org, for example, noted its mission as follows: "This site,
like many others, seeks to preserve the history and the heritage of the Persian
Gulf, and to prevent Pan Arabist dreams of eradicating Persia from the history
books." In 2010, Persiangulf.org was no longer available in its original form. It
announced on its site that its domain name "has been donated to the Persian
Gulf Advocacy group in order to promote the correct usage of the Persian
Gulf name." The hyperlinked PDF press release about the handover is even
toned and even tempered; it presents its cause while noting the importance
of treating all people with respect. While no additional information about
the group's activities are available on the site, the shift in rhetoric away from

assigning blame in inflammatory terms is promising. "Persiangulf.org Internet Domain Name Registration Press Release," March 10, 2010, http://per-
siangulf.org/201x/2010/03/12/domain-press-20100312.pdf.

17 The origins of the problem date to the early decades of the twentieth
century and until the termination of British presence in 1971, territorial conflict over areas in the Persian Gulf were primarily negotiated through the British. Since that time, both the ruling monarchy of Mohammad Reza Shah and
the subsequently formed Islamic Republic have had ongoing disputes over
the status of the islands. For more details on the history of the islands and the
dispute, see Amirahmadi (1996); and Mojtahed-Zadeh (2006a, 2006b).

18 Ali Akbar Mahdi, "Conscious Distortion," Iranian.com, http://iranian.
com/Dec96/Features/PersianGulf/PersianGulf.html#Distortion.

19 This ignores the fact that Iran has an Arab population of approximately
three million. As the Iranian Internet has matured and as Iran's global and
internal politics have become more volatile, both state officials and individual
Web site owners have begun to show more sensitivity to ethnic and racial
issues.

20 In a 2002 letter to Iranian.com, for example, a reader expressing anger at
Iranians who may have sympathy with causes in the Arab world (specifically
with the Palestinian issue) pointed to the Persian Gulf as an example of the
lack of reciprocity from Arabs, in the process eliding the boundaries between
the Islamic Republic, Arabs, and Islam: "It's the old problem of the incompat-
ibility of being a Muslim, and therefore allied with the sworn enemies of the
Iranian people, and being an Iranian nationalist. Make no mistake about it;
as a group, the Arab world is our historical enemy and Israel our natural ally."
Adrian Norbash, "Wake Up and Smell the Chai," May 30, 2002, Iranian.com,
http://iranian.com/Letters/2002/May/may30.html.

21 Amir N., "Persian (Traitors) Gulf," November 29, 2004, Iranian.com,
http://iranian.com/Opinion/2004/November/PG/index.html.

22 In 2004, Sharif Farsiweb, Inc. released the first standardized set of Unicode Persian fonts. For more on the company, its roots at Sharif Technological
University, and the impact of standardized Persian script on access to electronic media, see the company's Web site at http://www.farsiweb.ir/. Blogger
Hossein Derakhshan is often credited with pioneering the use of Persian on
blogs and teaching others to do the same. For a brief argument about the general importance of Unicode for blogging in Iran and for preserving linguistic
diversity, see Anderson (2005).

23 News.gooya.com is a well-known and popular example of a site that published the original works of a range of Persian speakers, especially the works
of older generations of Diasporic Iranians. The site, which was originally
published in Iran, was launched as Gooya.com in 1998 by journalist Farshad
Bayan. Bayan manually scanned Iranian newspapers and put them online,

allowing transnational access to Iran-based publications at a time when online newspapers were not yet common. For further background on the founding and development of Gooya, see Memarian (2004); and Saadi (2004).

24 In 2003, the Iranian authorities arrested Sina Motallebi, a former journalist for a banned reformist paper. Motallebi was the first of several reformist journalists-turned-bloggers to leave Iran after being arrested and harassed for their online activities. For an interview with Motallebi about his background and conditions of arrest, see Glasser (2004).

25 Examples could be found at www.parseek.com/arabian_gulf.htm; http://no-arabian-gulf.persianblog.com/; and http://pg.m2ix.com/. These sites more or less emulated the Web page that was designed to go along with the first Google bomb.

26 The original petition and the names and comments of the signatories can still be found online at: "Persian Gulf Will Remain Persian," Petition Online, http://www.petitiononline.com/persian/petition.html.

27 "Persian Gulf Will Remain Persian," available at http://persiangulf.20fr. com/, is one of the first Iranian sites to use flash video, but the video appeals to racist tropes. It tells a story of how Arab states bribed National Geographic into using the term "Arabian Gulf."

28 The reasons why the issue of prostitution figures less prominently in this period are not entirely clear, though it is almost certainly not evidence of a self-conscious decision by participants in the online debates on the Persian Gulf to avoid gendered/sexist language. Although some participants spoke out against racist or racialized undertones (as noted earlier), the gendered constructions of arguments about Iranian territories and the defense of Iran went unnoticed. Thus, the change may reflect awareness of conditions on the ground or changes in those conditions. In other words, perhaps Iranian women no longer constituted a significant presence as prostitutes in the United Arab Emirates in this period or perhaps they never had and the rumors faded over time. Despite the abundance of rumors and anecdotes, little reliable research is available about the recent history of Iranian prostitutes in the UAE or other neighboring countries.

29 http://www.petitiononline.com/persian/petition.html. The fact that the petition conflated all "Persian speakers" with the nation is noteworthy, since not all Persian speakers are Iranian and the first language of all Iranians is not Persian. This slippage illustrates one way that Iranian nationalism is conceptualized in the Diaspora.

30 For background on Iranian emigration and Diaspora populations, see Ansari (1992); Fathi (1991); Torbat (2002); and Yeganegi (2001).

31 Although the Iranian state's actions did not receive widespread attention from Diasporic Iranians online, it was covered in mainstream news sites. See, for example, "Iran Fights to Keep Gulf Persian," *BBC News*,

November 30, 2004, http://news.bbc.co.uk/2/hi/middle_east/4056543.stm. The state's actions were not completely unnoticed on the Iranian Internet. For example, a blog post in English reviewed some of the actions the government had taken and covers some familiar themes in the history of the attempts of Iranian Arabs to change the name of the Persian Gulf. The post was also noteworthy because it outlined the number of online tools the author relied on in joining the mobilizations around the Persian Gulf. While the blog is still accessible, the post under discussion, previously at http://babaklayeghi.blogspot.com/2004/11/arabian-gulf.html, is no longer available. However, the post can still be accessed at Babak Layeghi, "The Arabian Gulf?" Ghasedak Online, January 1, 2005, http://www.ghasedakonline.com/article.php?aid=1182.

32 Mohammad Ali Abtahi, "Khalij-e Hamishe Fars" (The Forever Persian Gulf), Webneveshteha, November 16, 2004, http://webneveshteha.com/weblog/?id=110060870.

33 The site sponsored by the Ministry of Culture and Islamic Guidance was previously available at http://www.khalij-fars.com/. In addition to linking to other sites such as the petition site, the page displayed a number of images, videos, and other content gathered in support of the name Persian Gulf.

34 Variations on the theme of "The Eternal Persian Gulf" figure prominently in popular songs and videos produced by members of the Diaspora. Given that anti-Islamic Republic of Iran sentiments appear in many songs by Diaspora composers, it is striking that an Iranian government ministry used the same slogan as some of the music produced in the Diaspora.

35 Hamid Soltani's animated video "The Always Persian Gulf" was available at http://www.khalij-fars.com/animation_files/24Khlije%20hamishe%20fars.swf and was archived on a page sponsored by the Ministry of Culture and Islamic Guidance page that was previously available at http://www.khalij-fars.com/animation/animlist.asp?cat=1.

36 Mohsen Taherian's animated video "Persian Gulf, as Always, Remains Persian" was previously available at http://www.khalij-fars.com/animation_files/23persiangulf.swf and was archived on a page sponsored by the Ministry of Culture and Islamic Guidance at http://www.khalij-fars.com/animation/animlist.asp?cat=1.

37 Fatemeh Esmaili's animated video "The Always Persian Gulf" was previously available at http://www.khalij-fars.com/animation_files/5Persian%20Gulf.swf and was archived on the ministry's page at http://www.khalij-fars.com/animation/animlist.asp?cat=1.

2 UNCHARTED BLOGOSPHERES

1 I use the term "nongovernmental" with caution here. Many self-described international nongovernmental organizations receive direct or

indirect funding from government entities. While commentators are often astute at pointing out the state connections of Iran-based organizations that claim nongovernmental status, foreign-funded organizations based in Europe or North America whose work focuses on human rights, civil society, and/ or the prospects for democracy in Iran often escape such scrutiny. A body of work has raised critical questions about the implications of hidden sources of governmental funding. See, for example, Rodriguez (2008). Similarly, others have questioned the interventionist drive behind the work of such organizations: That is to say, they have criticized interference in the domestic affairs of sovereign countries, especially when such interference is state funded and/ or is justified on the basis of values that are asserted to be universal. See, for example, Wallerstein (2006).

2 See, for example, Reporters Without Borders (2008); and Freedom House's annual publication *Freedom on the Net; A Global Assessment of Internet and Digital Media.*

3 The fact that the inconsistent and largely inexplicable restrictions force even the most hardline supporters of the government to use illegal proxies to access content online has raised some noteworthy debates in various arenas on the Iranian Internet. These debates, which are most visible in the realm of social media such as Friendfeed, where users of various political orientations can face each other in real time, reflect the diversity and contradictions of the Iranian Internet.

4 In the social media phase of the Iranian Internet (discussed in chapter 4), some individuals begin openly identifying themselves and/or their online projects with the ruling establishment as part of the state's response to what it called a "soft war" on its culture and policies.

5 For an example of this characterization of Iranian youth, see Mahdavi (2009).

6 Zahra HB originally began blogging on http://zahra-hb.blogspot. com/ with a mirror site on http://zahrahb.persianblog.com. The Persian-blog domain crashed in 2007 as a result of hacking, after which it changed its domain to Persianblog.ir. But this didn't affect Zahra HB, since she had moved her domain to the Zahra-hb.com URL it now inhabits in 2006.

7 "Mahdoodiat va Sakhtgeeri" [Restrictions and Strictness], January 5, 2007, http://zahra-hb.com/1385/10/restriction/, my translation.

8 See, for example, Yaghmaian (2002).

9 "Ehtemalan Eemanam Kheili Zaeefe" [Probably My Faith Is Very Weak], November 27, 2007, http://zahra-hb.com/1386/0, 2/weak-belive/, my translation.

10 http://zahra-hb.com/1386/01/virginia-killing/ 1/31/1386. The author has erased this entry.

11 Examples include the following posts: March 6, 2007, "Ye Matlab-e Kheili Toop" [A Really Awesome Issue], http://zahra-hb.com/1385/12/

toop-text/; January 22, 2008, "Hes-e Nostalgic va Yek Soal-e Chalesh Baran-geez" [A Nostalgic Sense and a Challenging Question], http://zahra-hb. com/1386/11/nostalgic-feeling-one-challenging-question/; and March 4, 2008, "Tafavothay-e Beyn-e Mohandessi va Modiriyat" [The Differences Between Engineering and Management], http://zahra-hb.com/1386/12/ diffrences-between-engineering-and-management/.

12 "Besmellah Rahman-e Rahim" [In the Name of God the Kind and Merciful], March 13, 2003, http://kelash.persianblog.ir/post/1/.

13 Political factions are extremely volatile in contemporary Iran, with constant shifts in alliances and re-alliances. Disagreements and splits among the Principalists were exacerbated in the wake of the disputed 2009 presidential election and during Ahmadinejad's second term.

14 See, for example, "Marhoom Estanli, Enghelab, Rafsanjani, Dovome-Khordadi-ha va Digar Hich" [The Deceased Stanly, Revolution, Rafsanjani, and the Reformists], December 13, 2003, http://kelash.persianblog.ir/ post/53/; "Anjoman-e Hojatiye, Bazgasht-e Hashemi, Felafel-e Arzeshi, va Yek Lakposht-e Dovome-e Khordadi" [The Hojatiye Society, the Return of Hashemi, Arzeshi Falafels, and a Reformist Turtle], October 25, 2004, http:// kelash.persianblog.ir/1383/8/; and "Barebachs, Movazeb Bashid, Tavalod-e Ye Suharto" [Guys, Be Careful, the Birth of a Suharto], May 12, 2005, http:// kelash.persianblog.ir/1384/2/.

15 "Vakonesh-e Sevom Beyn-e Abji Commandoism, Jamshid Aria, va Pinokio" [A Third Reaction between Female Commandos, Jamshid Aria, and Pinocchio], July 20, 2004, http://kelash.persianblog.ir/post/68/.

16 "Rabet-e Gholvegah-e Enghelab va Sardast-e Azadi" [The Relationship between the Kidney of the Revolution and the Upper Arms of Freedom], February 14, 2004, http://kelash.persianblog.ir/post/58/, my translation.

17 See, for example, the following post from October 12, 2005: "Naaleyn-hay-e Agha Seyed Mahmoud va Rooz-e Vasl-e Doostdaran" [The Sandals of Mr. Mahoud and the Get Together of Supporters], http://kelash.persianblog. ir/1384/7/.

18 "Be Soheil Madyoonam, Faghat Hamin" [I Owe a Debt to Soheil, That Is All], July 15, 2003, http://kelash.persianblog.ir/post/39/, my translation.

19 Hedayati was also critical of government entities, such as the state-run broadcasting services, for how they dealt with the documentarians. See, for example, a post he wrote after their release: http://kelash.persianblog.ir/ post/53/; "Anjoman-e Hojatiye, Bazgasht-e Hashemi, Felafel-e Arzeshi, va Yek Lakposht-e Dovome-e Khordadi" [The Hojatiye Society, the Return of Hashemi, Arzeshi Falafels, and a Reformist Turtle], October 25, http://kelash. persianblog.ir/1383/8/.

20 "Sal-e 81, Sal-e Veblogha" [The Year 2003, the Year of Blogs], March 19, 2003, http://kelash.persianblog.ir/1381/12/, my translation.

21 Kowsar provides an overview of her experiences with blogging in an interview with the Talabeh blog, a Web site dedicated to the blogging activities of seminary students: http://talabeblog.ir/n-1978.html. She also provided a link to this interview in the "About Me" section of her main blog.

22 The posts that fall under these categories can be found at "Nostalji" [Nostalgia], http://kosaraneh.com/category/nostalgia/; "Tarashovat-e Zehn-e Man" [Random Thoughts], http://kosaraneh.com/category/mentality/; "Roozane" [Quotidian], http://kosaraneh.com/category/daily. The last URL is no longer active.

23 See http://kosaraneh.blogfa.com/ and http://goldokhtar.parsiblog.com/ Author7283.htm.

24 Kowsar, "Zan Akhoond Mishi?" [Would You Marry a Cleric?] March 13, 2010, http://kosaraneh.com/1388/12/clergymans-life/, my translation.

25 The first through fifth prize winners would receive gold coins and the grand prize winner would receive a trip to Mecca to perform pilgrimage. The state's practice of giving prizes to promote online content that supported it in this period was not limited to the blogosphere. On June 11, 2003, for example, the official site of the Secretariat for the Coordination and Oversight of the Promotion of the Culture of Sacrifice and Martyrdom put out an open call for relevant contributions from readers, promising "valuable prizes" to the authors of the best articles. The secretariat and its Web site are examined more closely in chapter 3.

26 The now-defunct site of the festival and competition was available at http://www.imam-javanan.com/ from 2004 to 2006, when it was moved to http://www.emamvajavanan.com/, which is also now defunct.

27 In addition to the themes of the previous year, the 2005 competition included "The Mission of Youth and the Imam," "The Imam and the Sense of Responsibility of Youth," "The Imam, Youth, Innovation, and Creativity," "The Imam, Youth, Work, and Self-Sufficiency," and "Youth from the Point of View of the Imam." From the number of submissions noted on the site, the new categories were not very popular. The categories that yielded the largest numbers of submissions were "Open Forum" (311) and "The Imam in Your Words" (79).

28 The now-defunct site was previously available at www.khalij-fars.com.

29 The bureau's official Web site is available at http://rasaneh.org. It contains links to its reports.

30 Being identified or self-identifying as a Principalist blogger provides no immunity in the dangerous and constantly shifting sands of Iran's power structure. Although Principalist bloggers did not come to the attention of the international activists that usually agitate on behalf of Internet freedom, the state has filtered the content on their sites and has questioned or detained some of them. Examples include the cases of Omid Hosseini, the author of the blog Ahestan (http://www.ahestan.ir/), and Mojtaba Daneshtalab, author

of the blog Daneshtalab (http://daneshtalab.com/). While these cases were largely ignored by foreign and Diaspora media outlets and activists who usually cover instances of blogger repression in Iran, some in Iran—especially netizens of similar political persuasion—did discuss the situation of both bloggers. Both cases also received overage on Iranian news Web sites. See for example, "Chera Ahestan Filter Shode Ast?" [Why Has Ahestan Been Filtered?], June 14, 2010, Alef, http://alef.ir/vdcefw8f.jh8nei9bbj.html?75247; and "Mojtaba Daneshtalab, blogger Arzeshi Tabra-e Shod (The Principalist Blogger Mojtaba Daneshtabal was Exonerated)," April 29, 2012, Parsine, http://www.parsine.com/fa/news/61023/%D9%85%D8%AC%D8%AA %D8%A8%DB%8C-%D8%AF%D8%A7%D9%86%D8%B4%D8%B7 %D9%84%D8%A8-%D8%A8%D9%84%D8%A7%DA%AF%D8%B1- %D8%A7%D8%B1%D8%B2%D8%B4%DB%8- C-%D8%AA%D8%A8%D8%B1%D8%A6%D9%87-%D8%B4%D8%AF.

31 The announcement and outline of the ministry's plan can be found in the following report of the news Web site Alef: "Be Etela-e Koliy-e Darandegan vebsite-ha va veblogha Miresanad (All Owners of Web sites and Weblogs Are Hereby Informed)," Alef, December 30, 2006, http://alef.ir//content/view/3538/.

32 "The Complete Text of the By-Laws for Organizing Iranian Websites," The Homepage of the Organizing Websites and Blogs, The Ministry of Culture and Islamic Guidance,_http://www.samandehi.ir/help/regulation.html, my translation.

33 See, for example, Omidvar (2007).

34 The blog of Yek Hezbollahi, http://hezbollahi.mihanblog.com/, is no longer active. However, the full text of this post is available at "Mahdoodiat va Sakhtgeeri" [Restrictions and Strictness], January 5, 2007, http://zahra-hb.com/1385/10/restriction/. The quotation is my translation.

35 Alireza Shirazi, "Samandeh-i Site-ha az harf ta Amal" [Organization of Sites from Idea to Practice], December 4, 2006, http://shirazi.blogfa.com/post-48.aspx, my translation.

36 According to the many forums and technology news sites that reproduced it, the news Web site Alef is credited with breaking the story. The Iran ICT News Web site (http://iranictnews.ir/), for example, ran several pieces on Alef's findings.

37 "Interference in the Website of the Ministry of Culture and Islamic Guidance: Security Weakness Collars the Mastermind of the Organization of Websites Plan," *Donya-e Eghtesad* [World of Economics Newspaper], December 22, 2006, http://www.magiran.com/npview.asp?ID=1312538. This article included a strong analysis of the problems and inconsistencies with the ministry's plan.

38 Many bloggers wrote short posts about their refusal and/or placed the "I will not register" logo on their page. Participants included religious and

secular bloggers as well as Diaspora bloggers. In the case of the latter, of course, the stakes were lower, since the government had few ways to enforce its policies on sites outside Iran. Those outside the reach of the authorities likely participated out of solidarity and in an attempt to spread the word about blogger defiance. The following posts provide examples of noncompliance: http://arasoft.mihanblog.com/post/archive/1385/9; "Sitam ra Sabt Nemikonam" [I Won't Register My Site], January 8, 2007, http://mohsenphoto.blogspot.com/2007/01/blog-post.html; "Sitam ra Sabt Nemikonam" [I Won't Register My Site], January 24, 2007, http://azadlahijan.blogfa.com/post-167.aspx; and "Chera Sitam ra Sabt Nemikonam" [Why I Won't Register My Site], January 15, 2007, http://www.gozir.com/1385/10/25/samandehi/. Netizens also discussed their noncompliance in comments sections, including on sites that covered the government's proposal without opposing it. See for example, "Site va Sibzamini" [Site and Potato], January 17, 2007, http://jvadjon.blogfa.com/8510.aspx and "Etmam-e Hojat-e Ershad Baraye Sabt-e Site-ha" [The Ministry's Ultimatum for Registering Sites], Iran IT Analysis and News, March 8, 2007, http://itanalyze.com/archives/2007/03/post_3107.php.

39 According to *Kayhan*, only 840 blogs registered. The numbers *Kayhan* reported as well as an overview of the problems that confronted the architects of the registration plan are available on the Web site of the Dutch-funded online newspaper *Roozonline*: "Shekast-e Tarh-e Samandeh-i Veblogha: Sabt-e 840 Site az Sadha Hezar" [The Failure of the Organization of Blogs: Registration of 840 Sites out of Hundreds of Thousands], *Roozonline*, January 11, 2007, http://www.roozonline.com/persian/archive/archivenews/news/archive/2007/january/11/article/840–1.html.

40 Hamid Ziayee-Parvar, "Shekast-e Tarh-e Samandeh-i Vebsite-ha va Veblogha" [The Failure of the Plan for the Organization of Websites and Weblogs], Khabarnegar, January 14, 2008, previously available at http://www.reporter.ir/archives/86/5/005173.php, my translation. Ziayee-Parvar's harsh critique is particularly noteworthy given that his name appears as the main researcher for some of the ministry-backed studies on Weblogistan. For more details of Ziayee-Parvar's assessments of plans to register blogs, see Ziayee-Parvar (2008).

3 The Movable Image

1. The Tehran Bureau, a self-described "virtual" bureau that has an "editorial partnership" with PBS's *Frontline*, is a good example of a site that relied on and emphasized the importance of new media, especially moving images, in relation to the unrest in Iran. The site and its archives can be found at http://www.pbs.org/wgbh/pages/frontline/tehranbureau/. See also "Why Tehran Bureau?" (the equivalent of an "About Us" section) at http://www.pbs.org/wgbh/pages/frontline/tehranbureau/us/.

2. "The Imposed War," one of the officially sanctioned names for the war, affirms the state's narrative about its position as a victim of aggression and the defender of a violated nation. While this formulation may have been valid during the first year following the Iraqi attack on Iranian territory, it became less tenable after Iran refused Iraq's 1982 declaration of a ceasefire and the war continued for another six years. The other phrase used as an official euphemism for the war, "Sacred Defense," underscores the position of Iran as the entity under attack. The word "sacred" captures the state's attempts to articulate the war in religious and spiritual terms.

3. "Bozorgtarian Mostanad-e Defa Moqadas Sakhte Mishavad" [The biggest documentary on the Sacred Defense will be made], *Jam-e Jam Online*, February 12, 2012, http://www.jamejamonline.ir/newstext.aspx?newsnum=100803434924.

4. The list of such works is extensive. Examples include Seyyed Mohammad Anjavinezhad, *Hemas-e Yasin* [The epic of Yasin] (Tehran: Sourey-e Mehr Publication, 2004); Hedayatollah Behboudi and Morteza Sarhangi, *Pa be Pay-e Baran* [In step with the rain] (Tehran: Sourey-e Mehr, 2004); Maryam Baradaran, *Eenak Shokaran* [And now the hemlock] (Tehran: Ravayat-e Fath, 2007); Ahmad Dehqan, *Safar be Geray-e 270 Daraje* [Journey to the direction of 270 degrees] (Tehran: Sourey-e Mehr, 1996); Ahmad Dehqan, *Nagoftehay-e Jang* [Untold stories of the war] (Tehran: Sourey-e Mehr, 2004); Majid Gheysari, *Se dokhtar-e Gol Foroosh* [Three flower-seller girls] (Tehran: Sourey-e Mehr, 2004); Gholamreza Gholizadeh, *Ekhrajiha: Khaterat-e Shahid Haj Ahmad Moharami* [The expelled: The memoir of martyr Haj Ahmad Moharami] (Tabriz: Mousa Ghayoor, the Residential Chamaran Tabriz Co-op, 2004); Azam Hosseini, *Da: Khaterat-e Seyedeh Zahra Hosseini* [Da: The memoirs of Zahra Hosseini] (Tehran: Sourey-e Mehr Publishers, 2008); Hossein Neyeri, *Bozorg Mard-e Koochak* [The little big man] (Tehran: Sourey-e Mehr, 2004); Hossein Neyeri, *Farar az Mosul: Khaterat-e Shafaee Mohammad Reza Abdi* [Escape from Mosul: The oral memoirs of Mohammad Reza Abdi] (Tehran: Sourey-e Mehr, 2009); Ma'soumeh Ramhormozi, *Yekshanb-e Akhar: Khaterat-e Ma'soumeh Rahmarzi* [The last Sunday: The memoirs of Masoumeh Ramhormozi] (Tehran: Sourey-e Mehr, 2007); Fereshte Saeidi, *Qermez, Rang-e Khun-e Babam* [Red, the color of my father's blood] (Tehran: Boustan Fadak, 2003); Qassem Yahosseini, *Yek Darya Setareh: Khatarat-e Zahra Taa-job, Hamsar-e Shaheed Masoud Habib Khalaati* [A sea full of stars: The memoirs of Zahra Taajob, wife of martyr Masoud Habib Khalaati] (Tehran: Sourey-e Mehr, 2006); and Qassem Yahosseini, *Zietoon-e Sorkh: Khaterat-e Nahid Yousefian* [Scarlet olive: The memoirs of Nahid Yousefian] (Tehran: Sourey-e Mehr, 2008).

5. See, for example, Omid Mehdinejad, *Peesh az Oqyanoos: Majmoe-e Sher-e Moqavemat* [Before the ocean: Collection of the poetry of resistance] (Tehran: Bonyad-e Hefz-e Asar va Nashr-e Arzeshay-e Defa Moqadas, 2009);

Qeisar Aminpour, *Dardvareha: Gozid-e Ashar-e Qeisar Aminpour* [The pained ones: Selected poems of Qeisar Aminpour] (Tehran: Hamshahri Publications, 2007); Alireza Ghazve, *Qatar-e Andishmak va Taranehay-e Jang* [The Andishmak train and war songs] (Tehran: Loh-e Zarin, 2005); Seyyed Hosseini, *Gozid-e Sher-e Jang va Defa Moqadas* [Selected war and Sacred Defense Poems] (Tehran: Sourey-e Mehr, 2004); and Shahabeddin Vatandoost, *Cheshm dar Cheshm-e Fao* [Eye to eye with Fao] (Tehran: Nashr-e Shahed, 2010).

6. I would like to thank Narges Bajoghli for sharing her dissertation research findings on the Aviny Institute and its affiliated centers with me. Bajoghli's ethnographic research on the institute includes an overview of the complex web of funding that supports their work.

7. All of these appeared at the organization's main page at http://www.far-hangeisar.com/.

8. "Darbarey-e Ma" [About us], March 21, 2009, Farhang-e Eisar, http://www.farhangeisar.com/1388-08-18-16-21-24.html.

9. Another example of the vast resources the state dedicates to the war is the Foundation for Martyrs and Veterans Affairs, which has branches in all provinces. A March 1980 order of Ayatollah Khomeini established the foundation and required that the Parliament fund it from the national budget. The foundation was tasked with supporting the families of veterans and martyrs (e.g. by providing loans to purchase homes, subsidizing public transportation, providing medical insurance). It is also responsible for commemorating the lives and sacrifices of veterans and martyrs.

10. http://rasekhoon.net/.

11. http://www.rasekhoon.net/aboutus/, my translation.

12. http://www.tebyan.net/.

13. Bahman Mo'tamednia, the author of *Lalehay-e Asemani* [Heavenly tulips], a site dedicated to the war and its legacy, compiled a list of several hundred war blogs. See http://hezarvand.persianblog.ir. The list he compiled has been reposted on the *Rasekhoon* Web site at http://www.rasekhoon.net/forum/ShowPost-20146.aspx.

14. See, for example, the group blog Veblog-e Omoomi Ettela Resani Defa Moqadas [The general blog for information on the Sacred Defense], whose only posts are links to videos and digital films available for download. See for example the following posts: "Downld-e Tasaveer Video-e Namahang" [Download of videos], June 29, 2006, http://qorbat.blogfa.com/post-17.aspx; "Downld-e Tasaveer-e video-e Amaliyat-e Karbalaye-5" [Download of videos from Operation Karbala 5], June 29, 2006, http://qorbat.blogfa.com/post-12.aspx; and "Downld-e Tasaveer-e Video-e Amaliyat-e Beytol Moghadas" [Download of videos from Operation Jerusalem], June 29, 2006, http://qorbat.blogfa.com/post-11.aspx.

15. The main page for *Habil* is available at http://www.habil-mag.com/, which contains internal links to bibliographies and other resources on the Iran-Iraq War.

16. *Habil*'s independent and critical stance seems to have cost it in the end. In February 2012, the organ of the Ministry of Culture and Islamic Guidance responsible for granting publication permits informed *Habil* that the Press Supervisory Board had banned it.

17. Both Google video and YouTube launched in 2005. The popularity of the former soon overshadowed the latter, leading Google to acquire the latter in 2006 and eventually phase out its video-sharing service, instead providing a video search engine.

18. Rick Prelinger has considered features of YouTube that make it more desirable to users than traditional modes and sites for archiving and archival research. He identifies these as YouTube's "basic (if not overly sophisticated) social-networking features" (Prelinger 2009, 287). Similarly, Markus Stauff has pointed to the platform's "highly intermedial and remediating character" and its "principles of relating and comparing different items" (Stauff 2009, 241). These same characteristics—the ability to "favorite" videos and share videos, its mechanisms for juxtaposing different videos next to one another, etc.—are important reasons why YouTube was particularly attractive to users of the Iranian Internet.

19. http://www.youtube.com/user/aminamiens.

20. The two clips are available at "War, Iran-Iraq, Karbala," http://www.youtube.com/watch?v=Q0PURBbxinI; and "Iran-Iraq War," http://www.youtube.com/watch?v=KcTonGCz6c0.

21. RA is short for the Arabic phrase "Radiallhu Anhu," which means "may God be pleased with him."

22. "14 year old Iranian soldier (www.IranNegah.com)," https://www.youtube.com/watch?v=mkXdXqHqkds&feature=youtu.be.

23. The "About Us" section of Iran Negah does not provide any information about the site's funding or sponsorship. The site is unusual because it seems to be courting a non-Iranian audience. Its stated aim is to provide a more well-rounded image of Iran: "In Farsi, 'negah' means 'look,' and thus the name evokes a sense of the chance to peer through a sort of window into everyday Iranian life—something that most of us hardly have an opportunity to do. Iran Negah employs clips from Iranian media, raw footage, and historical footage to provide you with an inside look into Iranian culture, politics and society." See http://www.irannegah.com/.

24. "Iraqi Republican Guard T-72 Hunted Down," https://www.youtube.com/watch?v=ukGL2K9Me4U.

25. "Defa-e moqadas: Karbala Ma dareem miyaeem" [Sacred Defense: Karbala we are coming], http://www.youtube.com/watch?v=Q0PURBbxinI.

26. "Iraq-Iran War," http://www.youtube.com/watch?v=5KhJYC8JZOU&f eature=fvwrel.

27. The YouTube video was originally posted at https://www.youtube.com/watch?v=raAu_7Mdr70. YouTube has since suspended the account of the user for "multiple third-party notifications of copyright infringement from claimants."

28. "Chenge Del—çenge del—tenge del—koveiti poor," https://www.youtube.com/watch?v=kTSqZy960qc&feature=youtube.

29. See, for example, "Vadey-e Ma: Farda, Ashuray-e Sabz" [Our promise: Tomorrow, a green Ashura], http://www.youtube.com/watch?v=quWtc57XloU.

30. See, for example, "Koveiti poor—Yaran Cheh Gharibane," http://www.youtube.com/watch?v=czWe-iPc5uw&feature=youtu.be.

31. Examples of the war song "Yaran Che Garibane" being repurposed to challenge the Iranian state's violence can be found at "Yaran Che Garibane, Raftand az Een Khane" [Our companions left this home like strangers], http://www.youtube.com/watch?v=8WOR-NK2oZE; and "Koveitipoor -=- Gharibane" [New version], http://www.youtube.com/watch?v=kAqZz91YIPU.

4 SOCIAL MEDIA AND THE MESSAGE

1. Ari Berman, "Iran's Twitter Revolution," *The Nation*, June 15, 2009, http://www.thenation.com/blog/irans-twitter-revolution.

2. "Iran Protests: Twitter, the Medium of the Movement," *Time*, June 17, 2009, http://www.time.com/time/world/article/0,8599,1905125,00.html. For other celebrations of Iranian uses of social media during this period, especially Twitter, see Octavia Nasr, "Tear Gas and Twitter: Iranians Take Their Protests Online," CNN, June 15, 2009, http://www.cnn.com/2009/WORLD/meast/06/14/iran.protests.twitter/index.html; "Twitter Tells Tale of Iran Election," CBSNEWS, June 15, 2009, http://www.cbsnews.com/2100-205_162-5090788.html; Glenn Chapman, "Twitter Streams Break Iran News Dam," June 15, 2009, http://www.google.com/hostednews/afp/article/ALeqM5izPPeM-vxCZ3iW6Qi0-N7E-0qe-Q; and "A Twitter Timeline of the Iran Election," *Newsweek*, June 26, 2009, http://www.thedailybeast.com/newsweek/2009/06/25/a-twitter-timeline-of-the-iran-election.html.

3. Sue Pleming, "U.S. State Department Speaks to Twitter over Iran," Reuters, June 16, 2009, http://www.reuters.com/article/2009/06/16/us-iran-election -twitter-usa-idUSWBT01137420090616.

4. The Open Net Initiative's report "Internet Filtering in Iran in 2006–2007" is available at http://opennet.net/studies/iran2007.

5. Before the appearance of Balatarin on the Iranian Internet, the pioneering blogger Hossein Derakhshan created the Web site Sobhane, which translates as "breakfast" in Persian. With the slogan "the most important meal of

the day," the site allowed registered users to post links, thus adding a social component to news consumption. For reasons pertaining to the rise of Balatarin and Derakshan's shift away from reformist politics, which put him out of step with certain trends in the Iranian Diaspora, the Sobhane site fell out of favor with users. However, it played an important role on the Iranian Internet, especially because it marked the beginning of a transition to the era of social media.

6. The full statement is available at http://Balatarin.com/about. On the homepage of the Balatarin site, all materials save the "About" and "News" sections are in Persian. There is no "About Us" page in Persian, and the "News" section takes the reader to a Wordpress page entitled "Voice of Balatarin." It is not clear why this material is in English, but it may be necessary for public relations and/or funding reasons.

7. See Google's announcement of these changes at Jenna Bilotta, "Google Reader Is Your New Water Cooler," March 11, 2009, Google Reader Blog, http://googlereader.blogspot.com/2009/03/google-reader-is-your-new-watercooler.html.

8. See, for example, Sarah Perez, "Iranians Upset over Google Reader Changes," *Techcrunch*, October 25, 2011, http://techcrunch.com/2011/10/25/iranians-upset-over-google-reader-changes/; "10,000 Users Sign Petition to Save Old Version of Google Reader," *PC Tech Magazine*, November 1, 2011; and Adam Clark Estes, "The World Is Surprisingly Angry about the End of Google Reader," *The Atlantic*, October 25, 2011, http://www.thatlanticwire.com/technology/2011/10/world-surprisingly-angry-about-end-google-reader/44109/.

9. In 2011, Facebook announced that it was adding some editing options. Users could edit their posts within seconds but only if no one had commented on that particular post. See "Known Issues on Facebook," Facebook, April 28, 2011, https://www.facebook.com/KnownIssues/posts/217418684936503. In 2012, Facebook allowed users to edit their comments any time after posting them. "Facebook Now Lets You Edit Comments," CNN, June 22, 2012, http://www.cnn.com/2012/06/22/tech/social-media/facebook-edit-comments-mashable.

10. This feature and other aspects of Friendfeed were incorporated into Facebook after it acquired the service in August 2009. At the time, Iranian Friendfeed users expressed concern that Facebook would take the best features of Friendfeed and then close the service altogether. Thus, in addition to writing about the local conditions that affected their participation online (slowed-down Internet speeds, filtering, concerns about surveillance, etc.), Iranian users showed an awareness of the industry side of the platforms they used.

11. The echo chamber effect is easily created in social media and other Internet spaces because users can choose to receive information and/or interact only with information sources that confirm views they already hold. The issue of whether and how new media environments are particularly conducive to the creation of echo chambers has stimulated broader debates about their impact on democracy and social movements in general. The terms "cyberbalkanization" or merely "balkanization" have also been used to describe and critique digital echo chambers and their implications. The actual and potential consequences of this process have been examined in various contexts, including in relation to collaboration in the sciences, current systems of democracy and education, and the fragmentation of information (Van Alstyne and Brynjolfsson 1996; Katz and Rice 2002; Putnam 2000; Sunstein 2007; Sunstein 2009; Weinberger 2007).

12. Ahestan, May 21, 2009, http://friendfeed.com/ahestan/f2e0c1a8.

13. See, for example, Ruhollah Mahdavi, May 26, 2009, http://friendfeed.com/ruhollahmahdavi/3d3d6883.

14. The now-private post was previously publicly available at http://friendfeed.com/youneskazemi/3ec59754; my translation.

15. The now-private post was previously publicly available at http://friendfeed.com/gerdbad/525e239d; my translation.

16. A discussion of the inadequacy of Ahmadinejad's patriotism was previously publicly available at http://friendfeed.com/gerdbad/551c2cf5.

17. The posts were previously publicly available at http://friendfeed.com/3rri/034bbb53 and http://friendfeed.com/nazlikk/888e0f81/via; my translation. Both users erased their public accounts and signed up for new ones following the election.

18. See, for example, http://friendfeed.com/ruhollahmahdavi/0758abc1/16-18.

19. http://friendfeed.com/shalakhteh/5dd1007a; my translation.

20. Some live commentary was provided on feeds at http://friendfeed.com/nazlikk/6ea61de3 (now defunct); http://friendfeed.com/exir/c5a32120 (now private); and http://friendfeed.com/fakahi/607fa610.

21. The full video of the debate was later made available on the Web site of Iran's state broadcasting channel at http://www.iribnews.ir/News/Video/192016_413987c0.wmv. The selection I've quoted is taken from an English transcript available at "Mousavi-Ahmadinejad June 3 Presidential Debate Transcript," June 9, 2009, http://www.irantracker.org/analysis/mousavi-ahmadinejad-june-3-presidential-debate-transcript.

22. The now-private entry was available at http://friendfeed.com/milad/fa339b92; my translation.

23. "Emrooz Olaviyat-e Keshvar Moghabel-e ba Jang-e Narm-e Doshman Ast" [Today, the country's top priority is to fight against the enemy's soft war], Fars News, November 25, 2009, http://www.farsnews.com/newstext.php?nn=8809041385.

24. For example, in December 2010, the president's representative to the Parliament, Hojatolleslam Mohammad Reza Tajaldini, speaking during a press conference at the National Conference on Soft War, stated that following Ayatollah Khamenei's call to action, the Institution for Soft War (Nahad-e Jang- Narm) had been established with the help of "the country's cultural and political custodians and the Office of the Supreme Leader." "Moaven-e Parlemani Reis Jomhour: Emrooz Olaviyat-e Keshvar Moghabel-e ba Jang-e Narm-e Doshman Ast" [President's Representative to Parliament: Today, the country's top priority is to fight against the enemy's soft war], *Rasa News*, October 12, 2010, http://www.rasanews.ir/TextVersion/Detail/?Id=87473&Serv=36.

That same year, speaking to reporters at the 17th International Festival of Media and Press, Yadollah Javani, the administrative head of the Iranian Revolutionary Guard's political arm, also repeated Khamenei's quote, adding, "the enemy's aim in soft war is to change people's beliefs and values but if the [Iranian] media are alert and enter the scene in a timely manner, they can successfully stand up to [the enemy]." "Sardar Javani: Bayad Sarasar-e Keshvar Aleyhe Jang-e Narm Basij Sharad" [Commander Javani: Mobilization against the soft war must occur throughout the country], *Emruz*, November 11, 2010, http://www.emruznews.com/print/2010/11/005021.php. Similar statements have been made by the head of the Police Forces and covered by the Islamic Republic News Agency, previously available at http://irna.ir/NewsShow.aspx?NID=30454438.

25. The most notable example of this is the Web site of Dabir Khane Daemei Moghabele ba Jang-e Narm-e Keshvar (The Country's Permanent Secretariat for Confronting Soft War), which is available at http://www.h-jangenarm.com/. Another example may be seen at the blog named Soft War, which seems to only republish articles on the topic printed elsewhere, available at http://jang-e-narm.ibsblog.ir.

26. Indeed, Nye agrees with Iranian officials about the potential impact of soft power instruments such as the media, with the major difference that Nye is enthusiastic about the effects of soft power on Iran: "In 1994 Iran's highest ranking cleric issued a fatwa against satellite television dishes because they would introduce a cheap alien culture and spread the moral diseases of the West. He also turns out to be correct. A decade later, mass demonstrations in Tehran followed the spread of private American broadcasts" (Nye 2009, 51).

27. The state's concerns about what it sees as an assault on the country's culture and values are more broadly an existential worry. In an overview of Iranian authorities' statements on "Soft War," Monroe Price has shown that officials see what they consider to be an attack on the nation's belief system and culture to be a part of a bigger project of regime change in Iran (Price 2012).

28. Examples of books published since the declaration that combating soft war was a priority include Ali-Mohammad Esmaeeli, *Jang-e Narm dar Hamin Nazdiki* [A soft war in this vicinity] (Tehran: Saghi Publishers, 2010); and Hossein Abdi, *Jang-e Narm* [Soft war] (Tehran: Daftar-e Nashr-e Moaref, 2010). The publisher of the latter is directly linked to the office of the Supreme Leader.

29. "Film-e Barnamey-e Raz: Bayadh-ava Nabayadhay-e Fazay-e Mojazi" [The video of Raz program: The dos and don'ts of cyberspace], Mobin Media, http://mobinmedia.ir/3038/%D9%81%DB%8C%D9%84%D9%85-%D8%A8%D8%B1%D9%86%D8%A7%D9%85%D9%87-%D8%B1%D8%A7%D8%B2-%D8%A8%D8%A7%DB%8C%D8%AF%D9%87%D8%A7-%D9%88-%D9%86%D8%A8%D8%A7%DB%8C%D8%AF%D9%87%D8%A7%DB%8C-%D9%81%D8%B6%D8%A7%DB%8C.html.

30. "Olaviyat-e Vezarat-e Ershad Hemayat az Asar-e Taleefi dar Hoze Jang-e Narm Ast" [The priority of the Ministry of Culture and Islamic Guidance is to support works in the field of soft war], *Mehr News*, November 2, 2011, http://www.mehrnews.com/FA/newsdetail.aspx?NewsID=1450765. The other priorities the deputy minister cited include works on the "Sacred Defense" (i.e., the Iran-Iraq War) and on "Chastity and Hejab."

31. "Safhey-e Shaksiy-e Hamidreza Gharibreza" [The personal page of Hamidreza Gharibreza], http://www.gharibreza.com/.

32. "Film-e Barnamey-e Raz: Bayadh-a va Nabayadhay-e Fazay-e Mojazi" [The video of Raz program: The dos and don'ts of cyberspace], *Mobin Media*, http://mobinmedia.ir/3038/%D9%81%DB%8C%D9%84%D9%85-%D8%A8%D8%B1%D9%86%D8%A7%D9%85%D9%87-%D8%B1%D8%A7%D8%B2-%D8%A8%D8%A7%DB%8C%D8%AF%D9%87%D8%A7-%D9%88-%D9%86%D8%A8%D8%A7%DB%8C%D8%AF%D9%87%D8%A7%DB%8C-%D9%81%D8%B6%D8%A7%DB%8C.html. This is a transcript of the show; my translation.

33. The video of the episode is available at "Barnamey-e Raz: Bayadh-a va Nabayadhay-e Fazay-e Majazi" [The Raz show: The dos and don'ts of cyberspace], *Raz TV*, http://raztv.ir/video+pa54ez4a1h. The audio of the full episode is available online at "Balakhare Resaney-e Melli Darbare Fazay-e Majazi Harf Zad: Barresiy-e Bayadh-a va Nabayadhay-e Fazay-e Majazi Dar Resancy-e Melli + Soot" [Finally the national media talks about digital media: An analysis of the dos and don'ts of cyberspace in the national media + sound], *Weblog News*, August 10, 2011, http://weblognews.ir/1390/06/mediablog/16316/.

34. A report of the interview with the minister, Hamidreza Babayee, is available at "Ketabhay-e Darsi Danesh Amoozan dar Jahat-e Mobareze ba Jang-e Narm Tagheer Mikonand" [Education books will change to combat soft war], 30Mail, August 9, 2011, http://30mail.net/news/2011/aug/09/tue/11275.

35. "Darbarey-e Ma" [About us], Jang-e Narm: Akhareen Akhbar va Ete-laat-e Hozey-e Amaliyat-e Ravani va Jang-e Narm [Soft war: The latest news and information in the field of psychological operations and soft war], http://www.psyop.ir/?page_id=525; my translation.

36. "Bayanat-e Magham-e Moazam-e Rahbari Darbarey-e Tahajom-e Farhangi" [The Supreme Leader's remarks about cultural invasion], Jang-e Narm, November 20, 2011, http://www.psyop.ir/?p=10604; my translation.

37. "Chalesh-ha va Rahkarhay-e Moghabele ba Natoy-e Farhangi" [The challenges and strategies for dealing with cultural NATO], November 27, 2011, http://www.psyop.ir/?p=10807; my translation.

38. Ibid.

39. "Afsaran Cheest?" [What is Afsaran?], Afsaran, http://www.afsaran.ir/static/about#about_4.

40. "Sardar Jazayeri Khabar Dad: Tashkeel-e Gharargah-e Jang-e Narm dar Setad Kol-e Neerohay-e Mosalah" [Commander Jazayeri announced: The formation of a soft war headquarters for the joint armed forces], Fars News, January 14, 2013, http://www.farsnews.com/newstext.php?nn=13910911001182.

WORKS CITED

Abdi, Hossein. *Jang-e Narm* [Soft war]. 2010. Tehran: Daftar-e Nashr-e Moaref.
Abecassis, Michael. 2011. "Iranian War Cinema: Between Reality and Fiction." *Iranian Studies* 44, no. 3: 387–394.
Akhavan, Niki. 2011. "Exclusionary Cartographies: Gender Liberation and the Iranian Blogosphere." In *Gender in Contemporary Iran: Pushing the Boundaries*, edited by Roksana Bahramitash and Eric Hooglund, 62–82. London: Routledge.
Alavi, Nasrin. 2005. *We Are Iran*. Brooklyn, NY: Soft Skull Publishing.
Altman, Rick. 2004. *Silent Film Sound*. New York: Columbia University Press.
Aminpour, Gheisar. 2007. *Dardvareha: Gozid-e Ashar-e Qeisar Amanpour* [The pained ones: Selected poems of Qeisar Amanpour]. Tehran: Hamshahri Publications.
Amirahmadi, Hooshang. 1996. *Small Islands, Big Politics: The Tonbs and Abu Musa in the Persian Gulf*. New York: St. Martin's Press.
Amir-Ebrahimi, Masserat. 2008a. "Blogging from Qom, behind Walls and Veils." *Comparative Studies of South Asia, Africa, and the Middle East* 28, no. 2: 235–249.
———. 2008b. "Transgression in Narration: The Lives of Iranian Women in Cyberspace." *Journal of Middle East Women's Studies* 4, no. 3: 89–115.
Anderson, Benedict. 1998. *Spectre of Comparisons: Politics, Culture, and the Nation*. London: Verso Press.
Anderson, Deborah. 2005. "Global Linguistic Diversity for the Internet." *Communications of the ACM* 48, no. 1: 27–28.
Ang, Ien. 2001. *On Not Speaking Chinese*. London: Routledge.
Anjavinejad, Seyyed Mohammad. 2004. *Hemas-e Yasin* [The epic of Yasin]. Tehran: Sourey-e Mehr.
Ansari, Maboud. 1992. *The Making of the Iranian Community in America*. New York: Pardis Press.
Baradaran, Maryam. 2007. *Eenak Shokaran* [And now the hemlock]. Tehran: Ravayat-e Fath.

Behboudi, Hedayatollah, and Morteza Sarhangi. 2004. *Pa be Pay-e Baran* [In step with the rain]. Tehran: Sourey-e Mehr.

Boroumand, Firoozeh. 2005. *Ketab Shenasi Defa Moghadas* [Annotated bibliographic study of the Holy Defense]. Tehran: Ghadyani Publishers.

Braziel, J., and A. Mannur. 2003. "Nation, Migration, Globalization: Points of Contention in Diaspora Studies." In *Theorizing Diaspora: A Reader*, edited by J. Evans Braziel and A. Mannur, 1–22. Oxford, UK: Blackwell Publishing.

Bucar, Elizabeth M., and Roja Fazaeli. 2008. "Free Speech in Weblogistan? The Offline Consequences of Online Communication." *International Journal of Middle East Studies* 4, no. 3: 403–419.

Burkhart, Grey E., and Seymour E. Goodman. 1998. "The Internet Gains Acceptance in the Persian Gulf." *Communications of the ACM* 41, no. 3: 19–24.

Cairncross, Frances. 1997. *The Death of Distance: How the Communications Revolution Will Change Our Lives*. London: Orion Publishers.

Carr, Nicholas. 2010. *The Shallows: What the Internet Is Doing to Our Brains*. New York: W. W. Norton and Company.

Christensen, Christian. 2009. "'Hey Man, Nice Shot': Setting the Iraq War to Music on YouTube." In *The YouTube Reader*, edited by Patrick Vonderau, Pelle Snickars, and Jean Burgess, 204–217. Stockholm: National Library of Sweden.

Christensen, Miyase, and Christian Christensen. 2008. "The Afterlife of Eurovision 2003: Turkish and European Social Imaginaries and Ephemeral Communicative Space." *Popular Communication: The International Journal of Media and Culture* 6, no. 3: 155–172.

Clifford, James. 1997. *Routes: Travel and Translation in the Late Twentieth Century*. Cambridge, MA: Harvard University Press.

De Groot, Joanna. 1993. "The Dialectics of Gender: Women, Men and Political Discourses in Iran." *Gender & History* 5, no. 2: 256–268.

Dehqan, Ahmad. 1996. *Safar be Geray-e 270 Daraje* [Journey to direction of 270 degrees]. Tehran: Sourey-e Mehr.

———. 2004. *Nagoftehay-e Jang* [Untold stories of the war]. Tehran: Sourey-e Mehr.

Doostdar, Alireza. 2004. "'The Vulgar Spirit of Blogging': On Language, Culture, and Power in Persian Weblogistan." *American Anthropologist* 106, no. 4: 651–662.

Doroodian, Mohammad. 1993. *Khoneenshahr ta Khoramshahr* [From the bloody city to Khoramshahr]. Tehran: Markaz-e Etelaat va Tahghighat-e Jang.

———. 1994. *Faav to Shalamche* [From Faav to Shalamche]. Tehran: Markaz-e Etelaat va Tahghighat-e Jang.

Enloe, Cynthia. 1989. *Bananas, Beaches, and Bases: Making Feminist Sense of International Politics*. Berkeley: University of California Press.

Eriksen, Thomas Hylland. 2007. "Nationalism and the Internet." *Nations and Nationalism* 13, no. 1: 1–17.

Esmaeeli, Ali-Mohammad. 2010. *Jang-e Narm dar Hamin Nazdiki* [Soft war in these vicinities]. Tehran: Saghi Publishers.

Fathi, Asghar. 1991. *Iranian Exiles and Refugees since Khomeini*. Costa Mesa, CA: Mazda Publishers.

Fuglerud, Oivind. 1999. *Life on the Outside: The Tamil Diaspora and Long Distance Nationalism.* London: Pluto Press.

Ghazve, Alireza. 2005. *Qatar-e Andishmak va Taranehay-e Jang* [The Andishmak train and war songs]. Tehran: Loh-e Zarin.

Gheysari, Majid. 2004. *Se dokhtar-e Gol Foroosh* [Three flower-seller girls]. Tehran: Sourey-e Mehr.

Gholizadeh, Gholamreza. 2004. *Ekhrajiha: Khaterat-e Shahid Haj Ahmad Moharami (Dayee)* [The deported: The memoir of martyr Haj Ahmad Moharami (Dayee)]. Tabriz: Mousa Gayoor, the Residential Chamaran Tabriz Co-op.

Gitelman, Lisa. 2006. *Always Already New: Media, History, and the Data of Culture.* Cambridge, MA: MIT Press.

Glasser, Mark. 2004. "Iranian Journalist Credits Blogs for Playing Key Role in His Release from Prison." *Online Journalism Review,* January 1. http://www.ojr.org/ojr/glaser/1073610866.php. Accessed November 30, 2012.

Gonzalez, Vernadette, and Robyn Magalit Rodriguez. 2003. "Fillipina.com: Wives, Workers, and Whores on the Cyberfrontier." In *Asianamerica.net: Ethnicity, Nationalism, and Cyberspace,* edited by Rachel C. Lee and Sau-Ling Cynthia Wong. New York: Routledge.

Hall, Stuart. 1990. "Cultural Identity and Diaspora." In *Identity: Community, Culture, Difference,* edited by Jonathan Rutherford, 222–237. London: Lawrence and Wishart.

Hine, Christine. 2000. *Virtual Ethnography.* London: Sage Publications.

Hosseini, Azam. 2008. *Da: Khaterat-e Seyedeh Zahra Hosseini* [Da: The memoirs of Zahra Hosseini]. Tehran: Sourey-e Mehr.

Hosseini, Seyyed Hassan. 2004. *Gozid-e Sher-e Jang va Defa Moghadas* [Selected war and Holy Defense poems]. Tehran: Sourey-e Mehr.

Jacobsen, Knut A., and P. Pratap Kumar, eds. 2003. *South Asians in the Diaspora: Histories and Religious Traditions.* Leiden: Brill.

Jami, Mehdi. 2012. *Khoda va Ensan dar Gooder* [God and man in Gooder]. Brentford, Middlesex: H & S Media.

Jenkins, Henry. 2006. *Convergence Culture: Where Old and New Media Collide.* New York: New York University Press.

Johari, Abbas. 2002. "Internet Use in Iran: Access, Social, and Educational Issues." *Educational Technology Research and Development* 50, no. 1: 81–84.

Kamari, Alireza. 2008. *Tariki Negari va Tarikh Negari Jang-e Iran va Aragh: Majomoo-e Maghalat* [Writing darkness and the historiography of the Iran-Iraq war: Collection of articles]. Tehran: Markaz-e Etelaat va Tahghighat-e Jang.

Kandiyoti, Deniz. 1991. "Identity and Its Discontents: Women and the Nation." *Millennium: Journal of International Studies* 20, no. 3: 429–443.

———. 2000. "The Awkward Relationship: Gender and Nationalism." *Nations and Nationalism* 6, no. 4: 491–494.

Katz, James Everett, and Ronald Rice. 2002. *Social Consequences of Internet Use: Access, Involvement, and Interaction.* Cambridge, MA: MIT Press.

Kelly, John, and Bruce Etling. 2008. *Mapping Iran's Online Public: Politics and Culture in the Persian Blogosphere.* Cambridge, MA: Berkman Center for Internet & Society.

Khiabany, Gholam. 2010. *Iranian Media: The Paradox of Modernity.* New York: Routledge.

Khonsari, Ketabchi Kaveh, Zahra Amin Nayeri, Ali Fathalian, and Leila Fathalian. 2010. "Social Network Analysis of Iran's Green Movement Opposition Groups Using Twitter." In *ASONAM 2010: 2010 International Conference on Advances in Social Network Analysis and Mining,* edited by Nasrulla Memon and Reda Alhajj, 414–415. Los Alamitos: IEEE Computer Society.

Khosronejad, Pedram, ed. 2012. *Iranian Sacred Defence Cinema: Religion, Martyrdom, and National Identity.* Canon Pyon, UK: Sean Kingston Publishing.

———. 2013. *Unburied Memories: The Politics of Bodies of Sacred Defense Martyrs in Iran.* New York: Routledge.

Kluver, Alan R. 2001. "New Media and the End of Nationalism: China and the US in a War of Words." *Mots Pluriel* 18 (August). http://www.arts.uwa.edu.au/MotsPluriels/MP1801ak.html. Accessed November 30, 2012.

Lal, Vinay. 1999. "History, the Internet, and the Hindu Diaspora." *Diaspora: A Journal of Transnational Studies* 8, no. 1: 137–172.

Lanier, Jaron. 2006. "Digital Maoism: The Hazards of the New Online Collectivism." *Edge: The Third Culture.* http://www.edge.org/3rd_culture/lanier06/lanier06_index.html. Accessed December 2, 2012.

Lerman, Kristina. 2006. "Social Networks and Social Information Filtering on Digg." *Proceedings of the International Conference on Weblogs and Social Media (ICWSM 07),* December 7. http://arxiv.org/pdf/cs.HC/0612046.pdf. Accessed December 2, 2012.

Lessig, Lawrence. 2001. *The Future of Ideas: The Fate of the Commons in a Connected World.* New York: Random House.

———. 2004. *Free Culture: The Nature and Future of Creativity.* New York: Penguin Press.

Mahdavi, Pardis. 2009. *Passionate Uprisings: Iran's Sexual Revolution.* Stanford, CA: Stanford University Press.

Manoukian, Setrag. 2010. "Where Is This Place? Crowds, Audio-Vision, and Poetry in Postelection Iran." *Public Culture* 22, no. 2: 237–262.

Marvin, Carolyn. 1988. *When Old Technologies Were New: Thinking about Electric Communication in the Late Nineteenth Century.* Oxford: Oxford University Press.

Mazahery, Mohsen Hesam. 2006. "Harfhayee Baray-e Nashnidan" [Words for not hearing]. *Habil: Nashriy-e Daneshjooyee dar Zamine Tarikh va Farhang-e Enghelab Eslami va Defa Moghadass* [Habil: A student publication about the history and the culture of the Islamic Revolution and the Sacred Defense] 1, no. 1: 4–7.

Mehdinejad, Omid. 2009. *Peesh az Oghyanoos: Majmoe-e Sher-e Moghavemat* [Before the ocean: Collection of the poetry of resistance]. Tehran: Bonyad-e Hefz-e Asar va Nashr-e Arzeshay-e Defa Moghadass.

Memarian, Omid. 2004. "Chap-e Matlab ta Marz-e Fahashi" [Publishing to the border of vulgarity]. *Yas-e Now Newspaper,* January 1.

Mercer, Kobena. 1988. "Diaspora Culture and the Dialogic Imagination." In *Blackframes: Critical Perspectives on Black Independent Cinema,* edited by Mbye B. Cham and Claire Andrade-Watkins, 222–237. Cambridge, MA: MIT Press.

Miller, Daniel, and Don Slater. 2000. *The Internet: An Ethnographic Approach.* Oxford, UK: Berg Publishers.

Moallem, Minoo. 2005. *Between Warrior Brother and Veiled Sister: Islamic Fundamentalism and the Politics of Patriarchy in Iran.* Berkeley: University of California Press.

Mojtahed-Zadeh, Pirouz. 2006a. "Disputes over Tunbs and Abu Musa." In *Boundary Politics and International Boundaries of Iran,* edited by Pirouz Mojtahed-zadeh, 305–318. Boca Raton, FL: Universal Publishers.

———. 2006b. "Legal and Historical Arguments on the Tunbs and Abu— Musa." In *Boundary Politics and International Boundaries of Iran,* edited by Pirouz Mojtahed-zadeh, 319–340. Boca Raton, FL: Universal Publishers.

Mortensen, Mette. 2011. "When Citizen Photojournalism Sets the News Agenda: Neda Agha Soltan as a Web 2.0 Icon of Post-Election Unrest in Iran." *Global Media and Communication* 7, no. 1: 4–16.

Mottahedeh, Negar. 2008. *Representing the Unpresentable: Images of Reform from the Qajars to the Islamic Republic of Iran.* Syracuse, NY: Syracuse University Press.

Nagel, Joane. 1998. "Masculinity and Nationalism: Gender and Sexuality in the Making of Nations." *Ethnic and Racial Studies* 21, no. 2: 242–269.

Najmabadi, Afsaneh. 1998. *The Story of the Daughters of Quchan: Gender and National Memory in Iranian History.* Syracuse, NY: Syracuse University Press.

———. 2005. *Women with Mustaches and Men without Beards: Gender and Sexual Anxieties of Iranian Modernity.* Berkeley: University of California Press.

Neyeri, Hossein. 2004. *Bozorg Mard-e Koochak* [The little big man]. Tehran: Sourey-e Mehr.

———. 2009. *Farar az Mosul: Khaterat-e Shafaee Mohammad Reza Abdi* [Escape from Mosul: The oral memoirs of Mohammad Reza Abdi]. Tehran: Sourey-e Mehr.

Nye, Joseph. 2004. *Soft Power: The Means to Success in World Politics.* New York: Public Affairs.

Omidvar, Kaveh. 2007. "Mohlat-e Do Mah-e Vezarat-e Ershad Baraye Sabt-e Nam Sitehaye Interneti" [Ministry gives two-month deadline for registering websites]. *BBC Persian,* January 1, http://www.bbc.co.uk/persian/iran/story/2007/01/070101_mv-ka-internet-register.shtml.

Ong, Aihwa 2003. "Cyberpublics and Diaspora Politics among Transnational Chinese." *Interventions* 5, no. 1: 82–100.

Paravar, Fahime. 1994. *Fehresti az Filmha va Videohay-e Jang-e Tahmili Araq Aleyh-e Iran Mojood dar Arshivhay-e Seda va Sima* [A catalogue of films and videos in the archives of the Broadcasting Services about the war imposed on Iran by Iraq]. Tehran: Soroush Publishers.

Pedatzur, Reuven. 2008. "Checking Public Support for Nuclear Policy—the Inevitable Results." *Contemporary Security Policy* 29, no. 3: 577–581.

Prelinger, Rick. 2009. "The Appearance of Archives." In *The YouTube Reader,* edited by Patrick Vonderau, Pelle Snickars, and Jean Burgess, 268–275. Stockholm: National Library of Sweden.

Price, Monroe. 2012. "Iran and the Soft War." *International Journal of Communication* 6 (2012): 2397-2415.

Putnam, Robert. 2000. *Bowling Alone.* New York: Simon and Schuster.

Rahimi, Babak. 2003. "Cyberdissident: The Internet in Revolutionary Iran." *Middle East Review of International Affairs* 7, no. 3. http://www.gloria-center. org/2003/09/rahimi-2003-09-07/.

———. 2011a "The Agonistic Social Media: Cyberspace in the Formation of Dissent and Consolidation of State Power in Post-Election Iran." *The Communication Review* 14, no. 3: 158–178.

———. 2011b. "Facebook Iran: The Carnivalesque Politics of Online Social Networking." *Sociologica* 3.

Ramhormozi, Masoumeh. 2007. *Yekshanb-e Akhar: Khaterat-e Masoumeh Rahmarzi* [The last Sunday: The memoirs of Masoumeh Ramhormozi]. Tehran: Sourey-e Mehr.

Reporters Without Borders. 2008. *Handbook for Bloggers and Cyber-Dissidents.* Paris: Reporters Without Borders. http://www.rsf.org/IMG/pdf/guide_gb_ md-2.pdf. Accessed December 2, 2012.

Rheingold, Howard. 1993. *The Virtual Community: Homesteading on the Electronic Frontier.* Reading, MA: Addison-Wesley Publishing.

———. 2000. "Community Development in the Cybercity of the Future." In *Web.Studies: Rewiring Media Studies for the Digital Age,* edited by D. Gauntlett, 170–178. London: Arnold Press.

Rodriguez, Dylan. 2008. "The Political Logic of the Non-Profit Industrial Complex." In *The Revolution Will Not Be Funded: Beyond the Non-Profit Industrial Complex,* edited by Incite! Women of Color Against Violence, 21–40. Cambridge, MA: South End Press.

Saadi, Sina. 2004. "Dar Amadha Hazineha ra Mibpooshanand" [The income covers the costs]. *BBC Persian,* March 12. http://www.bbc.co.uk/persian/interactivity/debate/story/2004/03/040312_la-cy-internetf.shtml.

Sabety, Setareh. 2010. "Graphic Content: The Semiotics of a YouTube Uprising." In *Media, Power, and Politics in a Digital Age: The 2009 Election Uprising in Iran,* edited by Yahya Kamalipour, 119–125. Lanham, MD: Rowman and Littlefield.

Saeidi, Fereshte. 2003. *Ghermez, Rang-e Khun-e Babam* [Red, the color of my father's blood]. Tehran: Boustan Fadak.

Said, Edward. 2000. *Reflections on Exile and Other Essays.* Cambridge, MA: Harvard University Press.

Sameei, Ali. 1993. *Karname Toseefi Hasht Sal Defa Moghadass* [Account of eight years of Sacred Defense]. Tehran: Nasl-e Kowsar.

Shakhsari, Sima. 2011. "Weblogistan Goes to War: Representational Practices, Gendered Soldiers, and Neo-Liberal Entrepreneurship in Diaspora." *Feminist Review* 99: 6–24.

Sheffer, Gabriel. 2003. *Diaspora Politics: At Home Abroad.* West Nyack, NY: Cambridge University Press.

Shirkey, Clay. 2011. "The Political Power of Social Media: Technology, the Public Sphere, and Political Change." *Foreign Affairs* (January/February). http://www.gpia.info/files/u1392/Shirky_Political_Poewr_of_Social_Media.pdf.

Sorenson, John, and Atsuko Matsuoka. 2001. "Phantom Wars and Cyberwars: Abyssinian Fundamentalism and Catastrophe in Eritrea." *Dialectical Anthropology* 26, no. 1: 37–63.

Sreberny, Annabelle, and Gholam Khiabany. 2007. "Becoming Intellectual: The Blogistan and Public Political Space in the Islamic Republic." *British Journal of Middle Eastern Studies* 34, no. 3: 267–286.

———. 2011. *Blogistan: The Internet and Politics in Iran.* London: I. B. Tauris.

Stauff, Markus. 2009. "Sports on YouTube." In *The YouTube Reader,* edited by Patrick Vonderau, Pelle Snickars, and Jean Burgess, 236–251. Stockholm: National Library of Sweden.

Sunstein, Cass. 2002. "MyUniversity.com? Personalized Education and Personalized News." *Educause Review.* 33–40.

———. 2007. *Republic.com 2.0.* Princeton, NJ: Princeton University Press.

———. 2009. *Going to Extremes: How Like Minds Unite and Divide.* New York: Oxford University Press.

Tapper, Richard. 2002. "Introduction." In *The New Iranian Cinema: Politics, Representation, and Identity,* edited by Richard Tapper, 1–25. London: I. B. Tauris.

Tölölyan, Khachig. 1991. "The Nation-State and Its Others: In Lieu of a Preface." *Diaspora: a Journal of Transnational Studies,* 1, no. 1: 3–7.

Torbat, Akbar. 2002. "The Brain Drain from Iran to the United States." *Middle East Journal* 56, no. 2: 272–295.

Van Alstyne, Marshall, and Erik Brynjolfsson. 1996. "Could the Internet Balkanize Science?" *Science* 274, no. 5292: 1479–1480.

Varzi, Roxanne. 2002. "A Ghost in the Machine: The Cinema of the Iranian Sacred Defense." In *The New Iranian Cinema: Politics, Representation, and Identity,* edited by Richard Tapper, 154–166. London: I. B. Tauris.

———. 2006. *Warring Souls: Youth, Media, and Martyrdom in Iran.* Durham, NC: Duke University Press.

Vatanabadi, Shouleh. 2009. "States beyond History: Translations beyond Nations." *Middle East Critique* 18, no. 2: 177–183.

Vatandoost, Shahabeddin. 2010. *Cheshm dar Cheshm-e Fao* [Eye to eye with Fao]. Tehran: Shahed Publishers.

Walby, Sylvia. 1996. "Woman and Nation." In *Mapping the Nation,* edited by Gopal Balakrishnan, 235–255. New York: Verso.

Wallerstein, Immanuel. 2006. *Universalism: The Rhetoric of Power.* New York: The New Press.

Weinberger, David. 2007. *Everything Is Miscellaneous: The Power of the New Digital Disorder.* New York: Henry Holt Publishers.

Werbner, Pnina. 2001. *Imagined Diasporas among Manchester Muslims: The Public Performance of Pakistani Transnational Identity Politics.* Oxford, UK: James Curry.

Yaghmaian, Behzad. 2002. *Social Change in Iran: An Eyewitness Account of Dissent, Defiance, and New Movements for Rights.* Albany: State University of New York Press.

Yahosseini, Ghassem. 2006. *Yek Darya Setareh: Khatarat-e Zahra Taa-job, Hamsar-e Shaheed Masoud Habib Khalaati* [A sea full of stars: The memoirs of Zahra Taajob, wife of martyr Masoud Habib Khalaati]. Tehran: Sourey-e Mehr.

———. 2008. *Zietoon-e Sorkh: Khaterat-e Nahid Yousefian* [Scarlet olive: The memoirs of Nahid Yousefian]. Tehran: Sourey-e Mehr.

Yeganegi, Ismail. 2001. *Mohajerat-e Bozorg-e Iranian* [The great Iranian immigration]. Tehran: Elm Publishers.

Yuval-Davis, Nira. 1997. *Gender and Nation*. London: Sage.

Ziayee-Parvar, Hamid. 2008. "Samandehi Veblogha va Vebsiteha" [The organization of websites and blogs]. In *Majmo-e Maghalat-e Technologihay-e Jadid-e Resane* [New communication technologies reader], edited by the Research Group for Social and Cultural Studies, 5–31. Tehran: Deputy Office for Social and Cultural Studies.

———. 2009. "Jang-e Cyberi dar fazaye shabakehay-e Ejtemayee" [Cyberwar in Social Networks]. *Resaneh* 78: 40–49.

Zittrain, Jonathan. 2008. *The Future of the Internet—and How to Stop It*. New Haven, CT: Yale University Press.

INDEX

ABOUT THE AUTHOR

Niki Akhavan is an assistant professor of Media Studies at the Catholic University of America.

CPSIA information can be obtained at www.ICGtesting.com
Printed in the USA
BVOW01s1512091113

335810BV00002B/4/P